Big Fat Cat AND THE GHOST AVENUE

Takahiko Mukoyama
Tetsuo Takashima
with studio ET CETERA

윌북

• 영어를 이해하는 데 굳이 번역문은 필요하지 않다는 저자의 뜻에 따라 우리말 해석을 싣지 않았습니다. 하지만
이 책을 다 본 후에 정확한 번역을 확인하고 싶다면 윌북 영어 카페에 들러주세요. 언제든 환영합니다.
cafe.naver.com/everville

ビッグ・ファット・キャットとゴースト・アベニュー
BIG FAT CAT AND THE GHOST AVENUE

Copyright ⓒ 2003 by Takahiko Mukoyama and Tetsuo Takashima

Korean translation copyright ⓒ 2014 by Will Books Publishing Co.
Korean translation rights arranged with GENTOSHA Inc.
through Japan UNI Agency, Inc., Tokyo and Korea Copyright Center, Inc., Seoul

이 책을 스르륵 넘기다가
해설 페이지를 보신 분들은 깜짝 놀라셨을 거예요.
엉뚱한 책을 산 건 아닌가 하셨겠지만,
이 책은 틀림없는 Big Fat Cat 시리즈 3권입니다.

아직 변화를 눈치 채지 못한 분께는 미리 알려드립니다.
이번 작품 〈Big Fat Cat and the Ghost Avenue〉는
지금까지와는 조금 다릅니다.
뭐가 다르냐고요?

답은 아직 비밀입니다.

그러나 한 가지만 기억해주세요.
이번 이야기는 다소 읽지 못하는 부분이 있더라도
신경 쓰지 말고 건너뛰면서 술술 읽어나가세요.
이번에는 그럴 차례입니다.
자세한 설명은 해설에서!

지금까지의 줄거리

어느 추운 겨울날, 사람 좋은 파이 가게 청년 에드 위시본은 하루아침에 집도 일터도 잃고, 어찌할 바를 모른 채 거리로 쫓겨난다. 수중에 남은 것이라곤 에드의 심정 따위는 안중에도 없는 뚱보 고양이 한 마리뿐. 고속도로 갓길을 따라 마을에서 떨어진 모텔을 향해 가던 에드는 고양이에게 샌드위치를 뺏긴 데다 지나가던 리무진 때문에 흙탕물까지 뒤집어쓰면서 점점 밑바닥으로 가라앉는 기분을 느낀다.

그러나 에드는 뉴 에버빌 몰의 광고판에 쓰여 있는 '빈 가게 있음'이란 문구를 보고는 어느새 뉴 몰의 입구에 서 있는 자신을 발견한다. 그리고 뉴 몰로 들어가 실제로 푸드코트에서 비어 있는 가게를 확인하자, 되든 안 되든 일단 오너에게 찾아가보리라는 결심을 한다.

화려하게 꾸며진 오너의 방에 들어선 에드는 보잘것없는 자신의 옷차림 때문에 더욱 위축된다. 게다가 하필 빈 가게 건으로 다른 손님이 와 있던 참이다. 그 손님은 제레미 라이트푸트 주니어로, 방금 전 에드에게 흙탕물을 끼얹은 리무진에 타고 있던 청년이다. 우락부락한 보디가드를 데리고 다니는 제레미는 마을에서 제일가는 권력자의 아들이자 새로운 파이 체인점 '좀비 파이'의 책임자이기도 하다.

기가 죽은 에드는 그 자리에서 포기하려고 하지만 오너가 에드의 순수한 마음에 호감을 품고 제레미에게 반론을 제기하며, 비어 있는 두 가게 중 작은 쪽을 에드에게 맡기고 싶다고 한다. 단, 오늘 문 닫을 시간까지 첫 달치 가게세를 지불하라고 조건을 단다. 가까스로 긴장을 가라앉힌 에드는 문 닫을 시간까지 한 시간밖에 안 남았음을 알고 부리나케 뉴 몰에서 교차로 구석에 있는 은행으로 달려간다.

꿈이 실현될지도 모른다는 흥분과 긴장을 안고 몇 번이나 넘어질 듯 에드는 필사적으로 달린다. 인생을 살며 지금껏 무슨 일에나 지각을 면치 못했던 에드는 이번에도 늦어버릴 것 같은 불안을 느낀다. 하지만 무사히 돈을 찾고 뉴 몰로 돌아오는 순간! 허기에 시달린 고양이가 에드에게 달려든다. 갑작스런 공격에 에드는 뒤로 넘어지고 그때 수상한 리무진이 빠른 속도로 달려와 땅에 떨어진 가방을 낚아채고 달아나버린다.

에드는 차에 치여 주차장 바닥에 내동댕이쳐진다. 겨우 몸을 일으켜보니 돈은 물론 고양이까지 자취를 감춰버렸다. 의식이 점차 희미해지면서 에드는 고양이를 애타게 부르지만 대답은 들리지 않는데…….

Big Fat Cat and the Ghost Avenue

빛이 있으면 그림자가 생기지요.
누구나 빛 가운데서 살 수 있다면 좋겠지만,
그림자 안에서밖에 살 수 없는 사람도 많이 있습니다.

에드는 자신이 지금껏 빛이 드는 곳에서
살고 있었다는 사실을 몰랐습니다.
그리고 빛이 다다르지 않는 곳에서도
열심히 살고 있는 사람들이 있다는 사실도.

이제 시간을 잃어버린 거리에서 빛과 그림자가 마주치려 합니다.
그곳은 세상에서 버림받은 사람들이 모여드는 곳…….
유령의 거리, 고스트 애비뉴에 오신 당신을 환영합니다!

Something was wrong.

The owner knew this before he got the call. Because the young man, Ed Wishbone, had not returned to the office. Maybe Ed Wishbone had been lying about the amount of money he had. Or maybe he had just changed his mind and walked away. Young people are sometimes like that, especially nowadays.

But the owner knew better. He knew an honest man when he saw one. Ed Wishbone was not a very sharp person, but he was definitely not a liar. And the fact that Jeremy Lightfoot's bodyguard stepped out of his office after Ed was not comforting at all.

So when the clinic called, the owner was not really surprised. He just rushed over there.

The clinic was at the west end of the mall, along a narrow
corridor between a hobby shop and a greeting card store. Inside
the clinic, the owner found a nurse standing in front of the door
to the examining rooms.

"Which room?" the owner asked.

"The one at the end of the hallway."

"What happened to him?"

"He was hit by a car. His wounds are minor but we're
worried about his head. He hit it pretty hard on the asphalt. We
want to send him to the city hospital, but he won't go."

"Why not?"

"I'm not sure. He may be confused from the shock. Said
something about looking for a cat. He wanted to leave but we
stopped him. He shouldn't even get out of bed yet."

The owner frowned and knocked on the door. When there
was no answer, he opened it. He was greeted by an ice-cold gust
of wind.

"What the...? Mr. Wishbone?"

Wind was blowing in from an open window. The curtains
were flapping against the walls madly. The owner ran to the
window and poked his head out.

"Mr. Wishbone!?"

The November cold filled the darkness of the parking lot.
The only light came from the half moon above. There was no
sign of anyone anywhere.

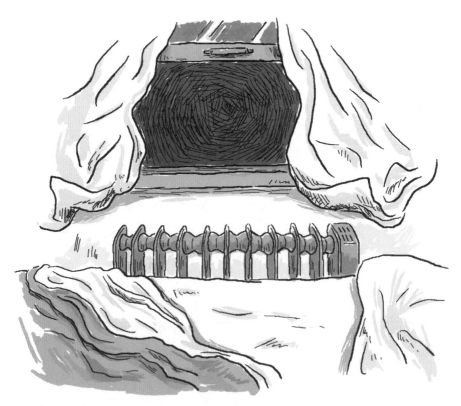

"Oh my God..."

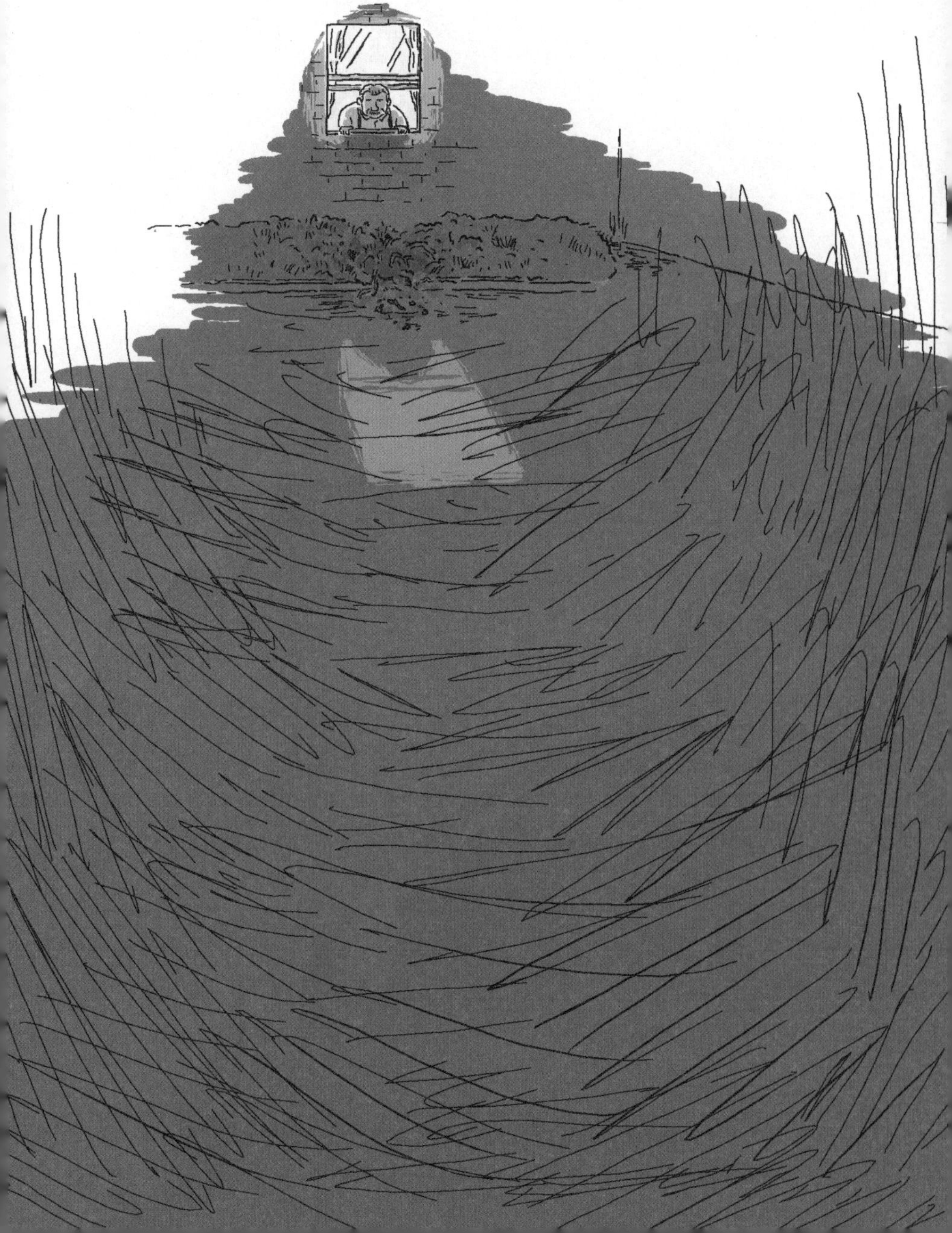

I was late...

I was late again...
(But it wasn't my fault!)

I'm cold... got to find the cat... so cold...
(Where am I?)

I'm a failure. I've always been a failure.
(It was the cat's fault!)

Got to find the cat...
(so cold... so cold... so...)

cold...

"Son, you're gonna freeze to death if you sleep here," a voice said. It was a soft voice.

Ed moaned. He was cold. His cheek was lying on something hard.

"Son, you really better wake up."

Ed stirred and opened his eyes. His memory was a blur. He didn't know where or when he was.

An old man was standing over him. The man had a long white beard, very old skin, and eyes that reminded Ed of Santa Claus. But it was a little too early for Santa, and Santa definitely didn't dress like this.

"Son, I don't know what the heck you're doing here, but you better wake up if you don't wanna become a damn Popsicle."

The old man moved slowly, pushing a baby stroller filled with books, magazines, and newspapers. One of the wheels of the stroller was missing. It had been replaced with the lid of a pot.

Ed got up with difficulty. He was lying in a dark, dirty street. The street was lined on both sides with buildings that had been closed for a long time. It was quiet except for the rattle of the old man's stroller.

"Where am I?" Ed said in a weak voice. His head was hurting like crazy.

"You don't know where you are?"

"I think... I... I'm lost..."

"Damn right you are. Everyone who comes here is lost. Pretty badly lost, as a matter of fact."

Ed looked around again. The moon overhead cast shadows into every corner. A gust of wind blew down the street.

Ed just wanted to sleep. He didn't want to walk anymore. He had never been so tired in his whole life.

The old man walked over to a giant pile of junk by the side of
the road. The pile was made of stuff that had been thrown away
when the street was still a part of the town.

"People have forgotten about this place. They call it 'Ghost
Avenue' now. We're just ghosts to them."

The old man picked a long piece of cloth that had probably
been a curtain some decades ago. He turned around to Ed and
smiled.

"We call it 'Treasure Island'."

Ed blinked. His blurry mind figured out that he was
somewhere on the northwest side of town, near the old mines.
The area had been busy during the twenties and thirties because
of the mining business. The barber from the shop next to Pie
Heaven had told him that there used to be a beautiful old cinema
here.

"Folks around here call me Willy. Professor Willy. Because I'm
the only one who can read," the old man said.

He handed Ed the long piece of cloth. Ed took it reluctantly
and wrapped it around himself. It smelled bad.

"I... I'm Ed," he managed to say.

The light of the moon played with the shadows. It was as if
the street was alive.

"Nice to meet you, Ed. Now follow me," Willy said, and
started down the street.

Ed followed Willy slowly, walking deeper into the darkness of
the street.

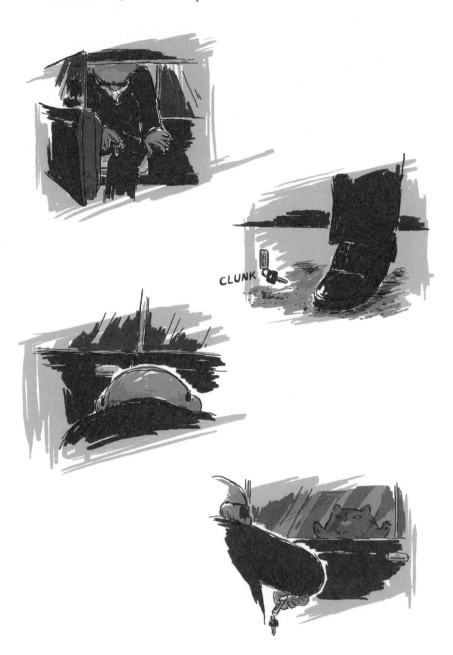

And back in Ghost Avenue...

"Here we are," Willy said, stopping in front of a unique two-story structure. Ed looked up at the building in wonder. It was a great big building.

The Old Everville Cinema really was beautiful. The barber had not been kidding. He had not been kidding about the 'old' part either. But the cinema still remained beautiful in a strange sort of way.

"This used to be a great theater back in the fifties, you know. Big screen, great flicks, buttered popcorn... But that was a long time ago. Now it's our home," Willy said as he pushed open the doors of the once-glamorous theater.

Inside, the theater lobby was ruined. The refreshment stand, the ticket booth, and the waiting area had been torn down, and everything had been replaced with piles of cardboard and miscellaneous junk. A few people were sitting there in the dark. The only light inside was a lantern hung from the remains of a chandelier.

A man rummaging through a pile of soda cans looked up and grinned at Ed.

"That's Frank," Willy said as he pushed his stroller through the mess. "He won't hurt you. Nice guy. Stinks, but a nice guy anyway."

"Howdy," Frank said to Ed, raising his hand awkwardly. He had no teeth. Ed just kept walking.

Willy walked across the lobby to a set of swinging doors that
were hidden behind a broken vending machine. Ed followed
cautiously, glancing around the whole time.

The main part of the theater was better preserved than the
lobby, except for one major difference. There was a big hole
in the ceiling. The blue half moon shined through the hole,
providing a soft light. There was also a warm red glow from a
small campfire that was burning directly underneath the hole.

"Here. Use them."

Willy pointed to a row of seats near the campfire. Ed sat down. He found the seats very mushy, but he didn't care. The seats were much better than the cold street outside.

"Well, you've met Frank, and that's George and Beejees. Louie's in that box over there, I don't know where Paddy is, but Marv's probably in the basement. He almost never comes out."

Ed nodded.

"What do you do for a living, Ed?" Willy asked as he tossed a few crumpled-up pieces of newspaper into the fire.

"I bake... I used to bake pies," Ed said, staring into the burning fire.

"That's a nice job."

"I lost my shop yesterday. I'm not a baker anymore."

"Sure you are. You're just a baker without a shop."

"Not just my shop. I lost my house, my savings, my bag, my whole life... all I have left is this."

Ed took his rolling pin out of his coat pocket. Somebody had found it lying near him in the parking lot of the New Mall. It always seemed to survive somehow. Ed tossed it on the ground.

It rolled straight toward the fire. It would have burned up if Willy hadn't reached out and grabbed it.

"Don't. This is important to you."

"No," Ed said. "I'm really not much of a baker. I just like baking pies. I was a mediocre salesman until last year. I quit my job, thinking I could become a pie baker because my mom used to bake great pies. She won a lot of contests. I thought maybe I was like her. But I wasn't. Stupid."

Willy stood by the fire, listening with a faint smile on his face. It was a smile worn by time and hardened, almost petrified, by the burdens of life.

Ed continued to speak, the light of the fire playing on his face.

"Mom always told me that life was like a blueberry pie. Sometimes it's sour but most of the time it's sweet. She said the most wonderful thing in life was to eat a good, warm slice of pie."

A tear formed at the corner of Ed's eye and rolled down his cheek.

"But she was wrong, you know. She died of a heart attack when I was in high school. From overwork. My father had left us the year before, and she'd had to work two jobs to raise me. One day when I came home from school, there was a slice of warm blueberry pie on the table. She was sitting in front of the oven, waiting for the pie to cool. But... she wasn't breathing. No last words. I never even said 'thank you' to her. I was too late. I'm always too damn late."

Willy walked up to Ed and held the rolling pin out to him. Ed shook his head, tears streaming down his face.

"No. I'm not going to bake any more pies. Life isn't a blueberry pie. A child can see that. It's... it's... more like a mustard pie."

"Look, Ed. You're going to get a good night's sleep, and then in the morning, you're going to go back to your life. You are not one of us. You have a life. Go back to it."

"You don't understand. I can't bake pies like my mother. I don't have it in me. I was only pretending I could."

"That's because you have no idea what a pie is really made of."

"Sure I do. I use the same things my mother did. I even use the same brand of flour. It doesn't make any difference."

"You had a great mom. She understood life well. She knew why pies were important. That's why she was a great baker."

"Pies are just pies. They're not important."

A long silent moment passed. Ed looked away while Willy
tended the fire. The crackling sounds of the fire eating into the
wood filled the air. Finally, Willy spoke. His voice was slow and
calm.

"Most of us haven't had a slice of pie in years, Ed."

Ed stopped wiping his tears. Still wearing that faint and
petrified smile, Willy continued, "Take Frank for example. He's
been here for more than ten years now. He's probably forgotten
what a pie looks like."

Willy gestured toward Frank, who was now near the campfire, looking for something in another big pile of junk.

"Why doesn't he just buy one?" Ed said with a rather guilty look on his face. "I mean, he could get a job, couldn't he? A pie is just a buck or so. Frank chose to be here... just like me. Bad luck, but it's probably his own fault. Anybody can buy a piece of pie. You just need to go out and..."

At that moment, Frank moved toward the fire. Ed suddenly noticed that he had no legs.

The tears came back all at once. Ed's face turned red and he covered his mouth with his hand. The tears streamed over his hand.

"I'm... I'm sorry. I didn't mean... oh no... I'm... I'm so sorry. I'm so confused... I'm really, really sorry..."

"No harm^(손)해 done, Ed," Willy said. "Frank was born on the street. Never knew his parents... A car hit him when he was twenty. Three hospitals refused^(거부하다) to treat^(치료하다) him and he ended up here."

The soft light of the moon enveloped^(싸다) the theater in its warm glow. The smoke from the campfire rose through the hole in the ceiling, up toward the sky, where it scattered^(흩어지다) among the clouds. The whole theater seemed like a gentle shelter for life.

"Ed... most of us here will die without eating another piece of pie... and we're the luckier ones. Some people never have the chance to eat pie. Not once in their lives. Some people have never had anything sweet, not in their mouths or in their hearts. For those people, Ed, life isn't a blueberry pie or a mustard pie. Life is just hell.^지옥"

Willy put the rolling pin down on the seat beside Ed and turned toward the campfire again.

"Sleep, Ed. Then go back. Bake more pies."

And it was a long night. The longest night of Ed's life. He was as tired as possible, but he still could not sleep.

He watched the campfire burn down.

He watched the moon shining in the sky.

And he watched the "ghosts" of Everville sleeping in their beds of garbage.^(쓰레기) Garbage that he might have thrown away.

He thought about all the pies he had baked. He thought even more about the many pies he had thrown away.

He thought of his mother.

He thought of his mother a lot that night.

Life is like a blueberry pie, Eddie. Sometimes it's sour, but most of the time, it's sweet.

For the first time in ten years, Ed remembered that there was something after those words. Perhaps the most important part which he had forgotten a long time ago.

And you know what, Eddie? It's always sweet if you eat it with the people you love.

Ed cried himself to sleep, and in the morning, he knew what he had to do.

When Willy woke up that morning, he couldn't believe what he smelled. It was the smell of fresh-baked pie. It was something he hadn't smelled for a long, long time. Willy got up and found his fellow ghosts standing around the campfire with Ed.

Ed was slicing up an apple pie.

"I'll be darned," Willy mumbled, his eyes wide with astonishment.

놀란 = "darned" gloss; 중얼거리다 = "mumbled" gloss; 놀람 = "astonishment" gloss

A metal container was hanging over the campfire, and more pies were baking inside of it. Ed saw Willy and spoke to him with a smile.

"I only had enough money for apple jam, so I guess it's not a genuine apple pie. And the crust is just graham crackers. But I did the best I could. I saved you a big piece. Here."

Willy took the slice of apple pie from Ed. It was on a piece of
wax paper. No fork, no napkin, but it was really apple pie.

"You were right. I guess I am a baker after all," Ed said.

Willy bit into the pie. It was sweet. It smelled of a long time
ago.

"Thank you," Willy said with a big smile.

Ed smiled back and said, "I'm going to get some more wax
paper."

"Sure. Oh, Paddy's probably out in front of the theater
sweeping. Please give him a slice too."

"Okay, I'll look for him," Ed said, and stepped out of the
theater.

But Paddy wasn't there.

Instead, Ed saw a big black man standing by the side of Ghost Avenue. The man's eyes were searching for something. Ed froze, the slice of apple pie held in his hand. He recognized the man from somewhere. The man looked like the bodyguard who had been standing behind the rich man at the New Mall's office. He also looked a lot like the man who had grabbed his bag.

At that moment, the man's eyes met Ed's eyes, and Ed suddenly knew what the man had been searching for.

Because the man had just found it.

Ed started to turn around, but it was too late. The man seized[불잡다]
Ed from behind and slammed him against the outside wall of the
theater.

"No words," the man whispered to Ed as he held him against
the wall.

Completely terrified[겁에 질린], Ed was unable to speak anyway.

"Understand?" the man whispered again.

Ed nodded desperately, although he could not understand
what was happening at all. He could barely breathe.

The giant black man stuffed[우겨넣다] a piece of paper in Ed's mouth
and said just two more words.

"Sign it."

Ed nodded at once. It was the only thing he could do.

The man let him go. Ed dropped to his knees on the ground, the pie falling from his hand. The man tossed a pen at Ed, and then started walking back to the limousine. Shaking all over, Ed picked up the pen and started signing his name. He couldn't think. He was too scared.

Before he finished signing his name, the sound of the limousine door rang in his ear. Ed raised his eyes from the ground and saw something that made his blood run cold.

The man was holding Ed's bag.

And something was stuffed inside.
Something very still.
Something shaped like a big, fat cat.

The man came back, and set the bag down in front of Ed.
Then the man picked up the paper. He checked the ^서명^signature
quickly, and without even a glance at Ed, started back to the
limousine.

Ed's heart was ^튀다^bouncing in his chest. He had the ^충동^urge to
throw up but he pushed it back. He remembered thinking that all
of his problems were the cat's fault.

"Oh, cat... I'm sorry... I'm so sorry..."

Ed slowly pulled the zipper of the bag open.

"AAAGGGGGHHHHHH!!"

Ed shouted as a very frustrated cat popped out of the bag
_{좌절한}
with a snarl and scratched his face. The cat leaped aside, and
_{으르렁거리는 소리}　　　　　　　　　　　　　　_{껑충 뛰다}
almost immediately noticed the piece of pie on the ground. The

cat took a giant stretch, and with the grace that only cats possess,
_{소유하다}
approached the pie and started to devour it.
_{게걸스레 먹다}

46

A smile of ^(안도)relief appeared on Ed's face, as he sat down on
the sidewalk weakly. The limousine had already driven away. Ed
leaned against the wall of the theater and let out a deep breath.
He still couldn't understand what that had been all about. It was
probably something about the vacant space in the mall, but he
didn't ^(신경 쓰다)care anymore. He was just glad that it was over.

The cat finished the piece of pie and looked up at Ed for
more. It seemed ^(불만족스러운)dissatisfied, maybe because the pie was not
blueberry.

"You understand a lot more than you seem to, don't you, cat?" Ed asked. A weak but sincere smile spread across his face.

"Blueberry pie is the only pie I still make from my mom's original recipe."

Ed looked into the cat's eyes. The cat looked back. It was a weird but pleasant moment, there on the sidewalk of a forgotten town. One cat and its owner, just staring at each other awkwardly.

Then, after a long silent moment, the cat burped.

HOPE

"Ugh! That's horrible," Ed laughed.

The cat made an annoyed face and started to look for somewhere warm to take a nap. It still seemed hungry. Ed's laughter echoed down the wide, empty road of Ghost Avenue, up and down, over and below, and on into the first glimpse of the day ahead.

Ed Wishbone knew that the rest of his life had begun.

and the story continues...

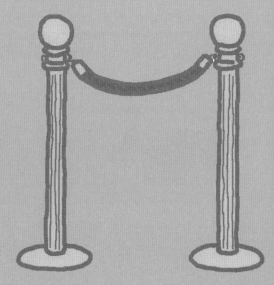 〈빅팻캣과 고스트 애비뉴〉 꼼꼼히 읽어보기

지금까지는 이 코너에서 본문에 대한 해설을 했지요.
2권 〈Big Fat Cat Goes to Town〉에서는
마무리를 짓는다는 의미에서 특히 자세한 해설을 수록했습니다.
하지만 이제는 충분하다고 생각합니다.

이보다 더 상세한 해설을 했다간
모처럼 막 재미를 붙인 영어가 또 지겨워질 위험이 있거든요.
'이해가 대충 된다', '조금만 더 하면 알 것 같다'
이럴 때가 바로 가장 바람직한 지점이지요.
'더 상세한 설명'을 하게 되면 도를 넘어서서 영어가 다시 복잡해지고 맙니다.

그러나 해설할 내용이 아직 있습니다.
여태 보지 못했던 새로운 방식의 해설이지만,
영어책을 읽을 때 알아야 할 중요한 내용이랍니다.

Big Fat Cat 시리즈가 선물하는 '또 하나의 해설'로 초대합니다!

이미 많은 분들이 느꼈겠지만, 이번 작품 〈Big Fat Cat and the Ghost Avenue〉는 앞의 두 권에 비해서 내용이 한층 심화되어 본격적인 이야기가 펼쳐집니다. 글자가 가득한 페이지들을 보고선 영어 문장을 줄줄 읽어 내려갈 수 있을지 걱정한 분들도 많이 있었을 거예요.

그렇지만 괜찮습니다. 걱정할 필요 없어요. 왜냐하면 어려워서 이해가 안 된다면, 건너뛰고 읽으면 되니까요.

"그럼 이야기를 제대로 읽었다고 할 수 없을 텐데……" 하고 불안을 느끼는 분도 있을 거예요. 하지만 우리말로 쓴 책이라도 그렇게 생각할까요? 영어라고 해서 특별히 여길 필요는 없어요. '건너뛰고 읽기'란 일종의 기술이라고 할 수 있어요. 이 기술은 결코 반칙이 아니에요. 건너뛰어도 이야기를 충분히 즐길 수 있답니다. 오히려 책이란 당연히 건너뛰고 읽어야 한다고 할 정도지요.

지금부터 그 이유를 설명해볼게요.

다음은 이번 작품 〈Big Fat Cat and the Ghost Avenue〉의 첫 페이지입니다. 이 페이지의 문장을 두 가지 색으로 구분해보았어요.

p.6

Something was wrong.

The owner knew this before he got the call. Because the young man, Ed Wishbone, had not returned to the office. Maybe Ed Wishbone had been lying about the amount of money he had. Or maybe he had just changed his mind and walked away. Young people are sometimes like that, especially nowadays.

But the owner knew better. He knew an honest man when he saw one.

Ed Wishbone was not a very sharp person, but he was definitely not a liar. And the fact that Jeremy Lightfoot's bodyguard stepped out of his office after Ed was not comforting at all.

So when the clinic called, the owner was not really surprised. He just rushed over there.

우선 연한 갈색 부분에 주목하세요. 분량이 가장 많고 중간에 위치해 있어서 중요한 부분처럼 보이지만 사실은 그렇지 않아요. 연한 갈색 부분은 원래 필요 없는 부분이에요.

소설은 어떤 언어로 쓰여 있든지 80~90퍼센트의 문장은 이야기의 뼈대를 세우는 데 그리 필요하지 않은 부분입니다. 연한 갈색 부분도 모두 이해하면 한층 더 재밌는 이야기가 되겠지만 이해하지 않아도 충분히 즐길 수 있어요. 말하자면 장식 같은 것입니다. 접시의 문양이나 커튼의 무늬처럼 있으면 더 예쁘겠지만 없어도 기능에는 변화가 없지요. 이 장식 부분에 무엇을 쓸까, 어떻게 쓸까, 이런 것들은 각자 작가의 개성에 달려 있습니다.

실제로 이야기를 이끄는 '원동력'이 되는 부분은 일부분의 문장뿐입니다. 이 예문에서는 진한 갈색 문장이 '원동력'에 해당해요. 읽을 때 이 부분만큼은 주의가 필요합니다. 그렇다고 갈색 문장 모두를 완벽하게 이해할 필요는 없어요. 계속 되풀이하지만, 어디까지나 문장은 상자와 화살표(혹은 등호) 부분만 중요하고, 부록 부분은 이해를 못해도 상관없어요.

왜 소설에는 이처럼 필요 없는 부분이 많을까요? 소설은 영화와 달리 이야기 속의 '시간'을 다루기 까다로운 매체이기 때문입니다. 영화의 경우 시각적인 장치로 시간의 흐름을 한눈에 알아볼 수 있게 하지만 글은 오직 문자로만 시간의 흐름을 나타내야 하므로 불필요한 부분을 넣어서 시간의 간격을 두는 것이지요. 언뜻 불필요해 보이는 문장과 표현이 들어가는 이유는, 기본적으로 바로 이 '시간의 간격'을 두기 위해서랍니다. 그러므로 극단적으로 말하면 읽지 않고 넘어가도 상관없어요.

예를 들어 다음과 같은 장면이 있다고 해보자고요.

[예 1]

　에드는 문 열기를 망설였다. 에드의 손은 땀으로 젖었다. 등줄기에서 서늘한 긴장이 흘렀다. 이 안에 드디어 찾아 헤매던 답이 있는 것이다. 에드는 결심하고 문을 열었다.

　연한 갈색 부분을 다 삭제해도 에드의 동작이나 이야기의 진행에는 지장이 없어요. 에드가 문을 열 때까지의 경과된 시간을 나타내는 '간격'을 두고자 에드의 심리 상태를 묘사하는 문장이 들어갔을 뿐입니다. 이번에는 심리 상태를 나타내는 문장 대신 그 '행간'에 쉼표를 나타내는 음악 부호를 삽입해봅시다. 읽을 때 쉼표 부호도 눈으로 따라가면서 보세요.

[예 2]

　에드는 문 열기를 망설였다. ♪ ♪ ♪ ♪ ♪ ♪ ♪ ♪ ♪ ♪ ♪
♪ ♪ ♪ ♪ ♪ ♪ ♪ ♪ ♪ ♪ ♪ ♪ ♪ ♪ ♪ ♪ ♪ ♪
♪ ♪ ♪ ♪ ♪ ♪ 에드는 결심하고 문을 열었다.

　쉼표 부호를 눈으로 따라가고 나서 마지막 문장을 읽어보면, 첫 번째 예와 큰 차이가 없다는 사실을 느낄 것입니다. 이처럼 '간격'을 두기 위해 삽입한 문장은, 설사 그 문장을 이해하지 않고 눈으로 스쳐 지나치기만 해도 충분히 기능을 하고 있는 셈입니다. 이것이 '건너뛰기'라는 기술의 실체지요.

　본문 6쪽 중간은 오너의 생각(연한 갈색 부분)을 주로 서술했어요. 즉 오너가 자신의 사무실에서 병원까지 가는 데 걸리는 시간의 '간격'을 표현하기 위해 넣었지요. 단순한 '행간'으로 두면 지루하니까 오너가 에드에 대해 느낀 감정도 보충하고 앞 권의 배경도 살짝 밝힌 것이랍니다. 물론 이 문장은 부록과 같아요. 기본적으로는 병원으로 빠르게 걸어가는 효과를 살리는

THE EVERVILLE TRAVELER'S HANDBOOK
에버빌 여행자를 위한 핸드북
로드리 해드슨 저　무코야마 다카히코 역

것이 최대의 역할이에요.

읽지 못하면 내용 파악이 어려워지는 '원동력' 부분은 실제로는 얼마 안 돼요. 시험 삼아 삽화를 보면서 진한 갈색 부분을 읽어보세요. 이때 연한 갈색 부분도 눈으로 스쳐가면서 오너가 뭐라고 중얼중얼 말할지를 상상해보면 실제로 모든 문장을 꼼꼼히 읽었을 때와 큰 차이가 없음을 느낄 것입니다.

소설이 지닌 이런 특징을 알아두면 훨씬 부담 없이 책 읽기를 즐길 수 있어요. 책 읽기에 익숙한 사람들은 무의식적으로 '건너뛰기' 작업을 하고 있는 것이랍니다. 모르는 부분 때문에 막혀서 리듬을 깨뜨리거나 모처럼 고조된 스토리를 멈추지 않고, 저자가 의도한 속도감을 잃지 않은 채 끝까지 읽는 것이지요.

아무리 재미있는 4컷 만화라도 한 시간 간격으로 한 컷씩 보면 지루할 거예요. 소설도 마찬가지예요. 재미의 절반은 치밀하게 계산된 '시간의 진행'에 있어요. 처음에 읽을 때는 되도록 사전을 펼쳐보지 말고 그 '간격'을 즐기라고 권하는 이유가 바로 이 때문입니다.

물론 사전을 펼쳐봐야만 할 때가 있어요. 신경이 쓰이는 단어가 있다면 사전을 들추어보세요. 단 귀찮지 않은 범위 내에서만 펼쳐보는 것이 요령이랍니다. 책은 즐기기 위해서 읽는 것이므로, 비록 영어책이라도 책 읽기가 고통이 된다면 앞뒤가 뒤바뀐 셈이지요.

만일 책을 끝까지 읽을 수 없었다면 그 이유는 다음 둘 중의 하나예요. 그 책이……

나의 수준에 맞지 않다. 난이도가 너무 높다.
혹은
열중할 수 없는 책이다.

어느 쪽이든 독자의 책임은 아니지요. 이런 경우 마음에 두지 말고 다른 책을 찾아보세요.

일단 한 번만 읽고 나면 다시 읽을 때는 그 소설의 진행 속도를 알고 있으므로 도중에 방해를 받아도 스스로 읽는 감각을 조절할 수 있어요. 이런 상태에서 사전이나 인터넷을 이용하여

PROFILE

인구	8,241명
상징물	새와 호수
명물	메기 요리, 커피롤
교통	시내버스, 시외버스, 로뎅공항까지 왕복 셔틀버스 운행

세세한 장치와 복선까지도 읽어내면 또 다른 재미를 느낄 수 있지요. 잘 쎄어진 이야기는 다시 읽을 때 처음과는 또 다른 새로운 즐거움을 선사해요. 이런 여러 가지 즐거움을 찾지 못한다면 손해가 아닐까요?

대화 장면 읽는 요령

다음으로 본문 7쪽의 문장을 보세요. 이 문장은 6쪽과는 분위기나 구성이 조금 달라요. 연한 갈색 문장은 여기서도 그다지 필요가 없어요.

p.7

The clinic was at the west end of the mall, along a narrow corridor between a hobby shop and a greeting card store. **Inside the clinic, the owner found a nurse standing in front of the door to the examining rooms.**

"Which room?" the owner asked.

"The one at the end of the hallway."

"What happened to him?"

"He was hit by a car. His wounds are minor but we're worried about his head. He hit it pretty hard on the asphalt. We want to send him to the city hospital, but he won't go."

"Why not?"

"I'm not sure. He may be confused from the shock. Said something about looking for a cat. He wanted to leave but we stopped him. He shouldn't even get out of bed yet."

HISTORY ~역사~

1800년대 후반부터 1900년대 초반에 걸쳐 스파이글래스 산맥에서 금이 나온다는 소문이 퍼지자 많은 사람들이 일확천금을 꿈꾸며 이 미지의 땅에 모여들었다. 금의 운반을 위한 철도 개통 계획이 수립되자 연결 기지로 번성할 것을 예상한 상인들이 현재의 에버빌 호수 주변에 차례로 숙소와 식당을 열어 작은 마을이 형성되었다.

한눈에 봐도 알 수 있듯이 대부분 진한 갈색 문장입니다. '간격'에 해당하는 연한 갈색 문장은 조금밖에 없어요. 그 이유는 이 페이지가 대부분 '동작'과 '대화'로 구성된 스피디한 장면이기 때문입니다.

제1권 〈Big Fat Cat and the Mustard Pie〉를 같은 방법으로 색 구분을 해보면 대부분 진한 갈색 문장뿐입니다. 왜냐하면 1권에서는 아직 영어 읽기가 익숙하지 않기 때문에 풍경 묘사나 심리 묘사가 없는 최소한의 문장으로 이야기를 진행했기 때문이에요.

그에 비해 이 책은 연한 갈색에 해당하는 '간격'이 꽤 많이 삽입된 거의 본격적인 소설이라고 할 수 있습니다. 영어 문장이 조금 어렵게 느껴질 수도 있지만, 꼭 문장의 완급을 즐겨주세요. 이 책을 통해 '핵심 문장이 어디인지' 보는 눈이 생기면 일반 외국 서적을 읽을 때도 강력한 무기가 될 것입니다.

보통 영어 소설에서는 " " 안에 들어간 대화 뒤로, 그 대사를 '누가 말했다(said), 물었다(asked), 속삭였다(whispered), 외쳤다(shouted)'와 같은 문장이 이어집니다. 이 경우 대화와 그 뒤의 문장은 그대로 연결돼요. 따라서 대화문 끝에는 마침표가 아니라 쉼표가 오지요. (? 마크나 ! 마크는 특별한 변화 없이 그대로 연결돼요.) 이 페이지에서 예를 들면 다음 문장과 같아요.

"Which room?" the owner asked.

the의 머리글자인 t가 대문자가 아니라는 사실에 주목해주세요. 대화문 뒤에 오는 이런 문장들은 대부분 건너뛰고 읽어도 된답니다. 대화문 뒤에 오는 문장은 해당 대화문을 누가 말하고 있는지 밝혀서 독자에게 혼동을 주지 않는 것이 그 목적이기 때문이지요.

영어에는 '나', '저', '저희'와 같은 자신을 표현하는 단어가 그리 많지 않아요. 남녀노소를 막론하고 누구든 'I'랍니다. 또 우리말처럼 연령과 성별에 따라 말투가 달라지는 법이 거의 없어요. 방언도 적고 어미도 변하지 않으므로 대화문만으로 개성을 나타내기란 거의 불가능하지요. 예를 들어 다음과 같은 장면이 쓰여져 있다고 해봅시다.

이 마을이 에버빌의 초석이 되었다. 그러나 지질학자들의 조사 결과 스파이글래스 산맥에서는 금은은커녕 동이나 주석조차 채굴할 수 없다는 사실이 밝혀지자, 철도 수립은 취소되고 선로만 무색하게 남겨놓고 개발 계획은 좌절되었다. 그 후 많은 이주자들이 이 땅을 뒤로 하고 떠났지만, 에버빌 호수 주변의 얼마 남지 않은 사람들을 중심으로 에버빌은 오늘날까지 조용한 발전을 이어오고 있다.

"주영, 내일 나랑 영화 보러 가지 않을래?"
"피곤해서 못 가겠어요. 김 선생님, 혼자 가세요."

이런 짧은 대화문만으로도 우리는 대화를 나누고 있는 두 사람에 대해 몇 가지 정보를 읽어 낼 수 있어요. 말투도 확실히 차이가 나므로 누가 하는 말인지 착각할 염려도 없지요. 그러나 이를 영어로 옮기면 다음과 같아요.

"Joo Young, would you go to the movies with me tomorrow?"
"No, I'm tired. Mr. Kim, please go by yourself."

이 경우 김 선생님의 성별 이외에는 모든 정보가 분명하지 않지요. 성별을 짐작할 수 있는 단어도 이름뿐이에요. 심지어 이름마저도 생략해버리면……

"Would you go to the movies with me tomorrow?"
"No, I'm tired. Please go by yourself."

이렇게 되면 이 대화만으로는 연령도 성별도 알 수가 없어요. 바로 이런 이유로 영어는 우리말보다 자주 '누가 말했다'와 같은 설명이 필요하답니다. 이렇게 뒤에 붙는 문장은 각본에서 대사 앞에 붙는 등장인물의 이름과 같은 느낌으로 쓰여요. 따라서 이름만 확인한 다음 건너뛰고 읽는 것이 오히려 자연스럽다고 할 수 있답니다.

ORIGIN ~이름의 유래~

여러 가지 설이 있지만 확실한 것은 없다. 다만 금이 나온다는 소문이 퍼지면서 마을이 번성하던 시절, 영원한 번영을 바라며 Everville이라는 이름을 붙였다는 설이 가장 유력하다. (이름을 붙인 사람은 에버빌 주변에 세워진 호텔 '파이어 위드 인'의 초대 경영자인 윌슨 P. 윌슨 씨로 전해진다.)

금기어는 되도록 피하자

pp.8-9

The owner frowned and knocked on the door. When there was no answer, he opened it. He was greeted by an ice-cold gust of wind.

"What the...? Mr. Wishbone?"

Wind was blowing in from an open window. The curtains were flapping against the walls madly. The owner ran to the window and poked his head out.

"Mr. Wishbone!?"

The November cold filled the darkness of the parking lot. The only light came from the half moon above. **There was no sign of anyone anywhere.**

"Oh my God..."

앞 페이지와는 정반대로 이 페이지에 나오는 문장은 거의 대부분 연한 갈색 문장입니다. 핵심 문장은 '오너가 문을 열었다'→'아무도 없었다'. 이 두 문장뿐이에요. 대화문도 나오지만 이와 같이 혼잣말인 경우는 이야기의 속도를 늦추기 위해서 사용되는 경향이 있어요.

마지막 오너의 대사 'Oh my God'은 미국인이 놀랄 때 자연스럽게 하는 말입니다. 영어에는 감정을 표현하는 단어가 풍부해요. 그러나 'Oh my God'처럼 평상시에는 잘 사용하지 않고 특별한 상황에서만 쓰이는 표현들이 있습니다. 이런 표현은 강렬한 인상을 주긴 하지만, 그리 권하고 싶지는 않아요. 무심코 사용했다가는 신용을 잃을 수도 있고 엉뚱한 오해를 불러일으킬 수도 있기 때문이죠. 그러나 영어를 배우기 위해서는 피할 수 없는 요소이기도 해요. 이런 표현은 많이 있지만, 여기서는 특히 많이 사용되는 표현 하나만 소개할게요.

우리도 길을 가다 껌을 밟거나 하면 불쑥 '에잇'이라는 말이 튀어나올 때가 있지요? 바로 이런 경우에 쓰는 영어 표현이 'shit'입니다. 의미도 사용하는 타이밍도 같지만, 의식적으로는

1920년대부터 1930년대에 걸쳐 추진되던 광산 발굴이 중지되자, 화가 난 마을 사람들이 '처음부터 존재하지 않았던 꿈속의 마을'이라는 의미로 이름에 N자를 붙여 Neverville이라고 부르던 시기도 있었다. (이는 강의 이름으로 현재까지 남아 있다.) 그 후 1950년대에 설립된 시의회가 '이미지가 나쁘다'는 이유로 다시 Everville이란 이름을 쓰기로 결정하여 현재에 이르고 있다.

사용하지 마세요. 이런 표현은 알아두면 손해는 아니지만 고상한 표현은 아니에요. 자신도 모르게 입에서 튀어나온 경우라면 어쩔 수 없지만, 외국인이 무리해서 쓰면 악의를 담은 표현으로 받아들여지기 십상입니다. 강한 놀람을 영어로 표현하고픈 순간이 되면 우선 오너와 마찬가지로 'Oh my (God)'을 작게 중얼거리는 정도로 시작해보세요.

강조할 때 쓰는 표현들: so와 very 중 어느 쪽이 강도가 강할까요?

pp.10-13
I was late...
I was late again...
(But it wasn't my fault!)
I'm cold... got to find the cat... so cold...
(Where am I?)
I'm a faliure. I've always been a failure.
(It was the cat's fault!)
Got to find the cat...
(so cold... so cold... so...)
cold...

이 페이지는 에드의 생각이 단편적으로 떠올랐다가 사라지는 장면입니다. 혼란 상태에 빠져 생각이 정리되지 않는 에드가 마음속으로 자신과 싸움을 벌이고 있는지도 몰라요.

여기서 주목해야 할 건 so라는 단어의 쓰임입니다. 이 단어는 다른 화장품 앞에 붙어서 '매우 ~하다'라는 의미를 더해줘요.

GEOGRAPHY ~지리~

거대한 산맥 사이에 위치한 에버빌은 여름에는 서늘하다. 하지만 겨울에는 심한 눈보라가 몰아치고, 스파이글래스 산맥에서 불어오는 바람이 끊임없이 마을의 상공으로 흘러가므로 구름의 흐름이 빨라지며 1년 중 가장 하늘이 높아진다. 당초 마을의 중심부는 에버빌 호수 주변 지역이었지만, 태풍이 올 때마다 호수가 범람해서 현재는 호수에서 서쪽으로 10마일 정도 이동한 지역이 마을의 중심부다.

영어에는 이처럼 의미를 강조하는 단어가 많아요. cold를 예로 들어보면 바로 떠오르는 단어만 해도 colder, coldest, very cold, really cold, so cold, too cold, damn cold와 같이 정말 다양하지요. 그럼 어떤 표현이 더욱 강도가 강할까요? 이들 표현은 각각 어떤 상황에서 쓰일까요? 물론 사용하는 사람의 성향에 따라 달라지므로 딱히 정해진 법칙은 없지만, 참고로 일반적인 이미지를 정리해보았어요. 재미 삼아 한번 훑어보세요.

[-er]

뭔가 비교의 대상이 있어서 그보다 더한 경우에 사용하므로 단순히 '비교'를 할 때 쓰는 단어로 생각하기 쉽지만, 실제로는 '-er than ~'이라는 형태로 비유할 때 쓰이는 경우가 일반적이에요. 예를 들어 'colder than winter'라면 '겨울보다도 추운', 다시 말해 '매우 추운'이라는 의미가 돼요. ~을 강렬한 단어로 채우면 -est나 so보다도 훨씬 강도 높은 강조를 할 수 있어요.

Our house is colder. (냉정. 상대를 설득하고 있는 인상)
Our house is colder than the north pole. (냉정하고 강경한 의사 표현)

[-est]

아마 강조 표현 중 가장 사용 빈도가 낮은 형태일 것입니다. '가장 강도가 강하다'고 알려진 최대의 강조 표현이지만, 오히려 -er과 마찬가지로 비유로 쓰일 때가 많아요. 우리말로 과장해서 표현할 때도 '세계에서 가장 ~하다'라는 표현을 쓰듯이 이 표현도 코믹한 느낌을 줍니다. 그래서 -est는 약간 유치한 느낌이 있는 강조예요.

Our house is the coldest. (단정적인 과장. 코믹한 인상)

[very]

가장 표준적이고 특징이 없어요. 보편적으로 사용할 수 있는 '강조'지요. 너무 흔히 쓰는 탓에 그다지 강렬한 인상은 없어요. 회화 중에 very를 강하게 발음하면 조금은 효과를 줄 수는 있지만, 문장 중에서는 그렇게 할 수도 없기 때문에 결국 지나쳐버리기 일쑤입니다.

에버빌은 마을의 중심부를 남북으로 달리는 밸리 밀즈 도로(Valley Mills Drive)를 기준으로 크게 구시가지와 뉴타운으로 나뉜다. 최근에는 마을 주변을 휴양지로 재개발하려는 계획(For-Everville Campaign)을 세우고 구시가지에 많이 있는 문 닫은 가게들을 철거하려고 했으나 예전부터 마을을 지켜온 주민들의 끈질긴 반대에 부딪혀 진행이 늦어지고 있다.

Our house is very cold. (단순히 평균보다 춥다는 인상)

[really]

상대가 말하는 사람의 생각만큼 대단하게 여기지 않을 때 '아냐, 정말 대단했어'라고 하듯이 재확인의 의미를 담아 사용합니다.

Our house is really cold. (제일 춥지는 않지만 정말 춥다는 인상)

[so]

매우 감정적인 강조입니다. '정말 ~해서 어떻게 할 수가 없다'와 같이 상당히 격양된 기분이 전달되지요. 일반적으로 그렇다는 뜻이 아니라 말하는 당사자에게 '엄청나게 ~한' 경우에 사용해요.

Our house is so cold. (주관적. 절실한 상황)

[too]

여러 '강조' 표현 중에서 유일하게 부정적인 뉘앙스를 담고 있는 단어입니다. '대단하기는 한데 도가 지나치다'라는 마이너스 의미를 함축하고 있어요.

Our house is too cold. (한계를 넘은 인상. so에 비하면 어딘지 냉정해요)

[damn]

앞에 나왔던 shit과 마찬가지로 '금기어' 중의 하나입니다. 함부로 사용해선 안 된다는 전제가 있는 만큼 '분노'나 '자포자기'의 감정이 강하게 표출돼요. 내뱉는 말투라고 할 수 있지요.

Our house is damn cold. (분노를 동반한 공격적인 인상. 강렬한 인상을 주지만 상대에게 부정적인 인상을 줘요.)

'강조'하기 위해 사용하는 표현은 이외에도 많이 있어요. 이보다 더 강하게 강조하는 방법도 있지만 일단 이 정도만 알아두면 충분합니다.

TRAVEL ~관광~

에버빌의 관광지로는 여름에는 메기 요리로 유명한 에브리 호수(Lake Every), 겨울에는 스키 관광객으로 붐비는 스파이글래스 산맥이 대표적이에요. 캠프 시설과 스키 산장들은 50년 전에 만들어진 건물이라 역사의 자취를 느낄 수도 있지만, 대부분 오래되고 낡았어요. 그래서 For-Everville Campaign의 일환으로 대형 레저 시설을 건설 중에 있고, 이미 뉴 에버빌 몰을 비롯한 일부 시설은 이주를 시작했다.

이야기를 끌고 나가는 원동력: 대화

이야기를 끌고 나가는 중요한 요소는 단연 대화문입니다. 일단 대화가 나오기만 하면 이야기는 생동감이 감돌면서 앞으로 나아가는 느낌을 줘요. 또 대화문이 이어지면 이야기의 리듬이 살아나서 읽기도 쉬워집니다. 이 책에서도 14~19쪽은 에드와 윌리의 대화를 중심으로 장면이 진행됩니다. '대화'와 '동작' 사이에 '주변 풍경에 대한 설명'이 삽입된 전통적인 문장이지요. 이런 경우는 전자가 '원동력(진한 갈색)', 후자가 '간격(연한 갈색)'이 되는 것이 일반적입니다.

여기에서는 진한 갈색과 연한 갈색이 어떤 역할을 하는지 보기 위해 일단 색으로 구분해보았습니다. 다소 긴 문장이지만 문장의 연결과 그 역할들을 느끼면서 쭉 훑어보세요.

p.14

"Son, you're gonna freeze to death if you sleep here," a voice said. It was a soft voice.

Ed moaned. He was cold. His cheek was lying on something hard.

"Son, you really better wake up."

Ed stirred and opened his eyes. His memory was a blur. He didn't know where or when he was.

An old man was standing over him. The man had a long white beard, very old skin, and eyes that reminded Ed of Santa Claus. But it was a little too early for Santa, and Santa definitely didn't dress like this.

p.15

"Son, I don't know what the heck you're doing here, but you better wake up if you don't wanna become a damn Popsicle."

The old man moved slowly, pushing a baby stroller filled with books,

이외에 볼 만한 관광 코스로는 에브리 호수 유람선이 있다. 세 시간에 걸쳐 느긋하게 호수의 풍광을 구경하다 보면 글래스 뷰(GLASS VIEW)에 이른다. 글래스 뷰는 이웃마을과 함께 공동으로 설립한 에버빌 스탠드 포인트 지역 대학의 캠퍼스로 질푸른 녹음이 볼 만하다. 색다른 곳으로는 광산 채굴이 헛소동으로 끝나버렸음에도 불구하고 그 실패의 행적을 전시한 러시로 광산 박물관이 있다.

magazines, and newspapers. One of the wheels of the stroller was missing. It had been replaced with the lid of a pot.

Ed got up with difficulty. He was lying in a dark, dirty street. The street was lined on both sides with buildings that had been closed for a long time. It was quiet except for the rattle of the old man's stroller.

p.16

"Where am I?" Ed said in a weak voice. His head was hurting like crazy.

"You don't know where you are?"

"I think... I... I'm lost..."

"Damn right you are. Everyone who comes here is lost. Pretty badly lost, as a matter of fact."

Ed looked around again. The moon overhead cast shadows into every corner. A gust of wind blew down the street.

Ed just wanted to sleep. He didn't want to walk anymore. He had never been so tired in his whole life.

p.18

The old man walked over to a giant pile of junk by the side of the road. The pile was made of stuff that had been thrown away when the street was still a part of the town.

"People have forgotten about this place. They call it 'Ghost Avenue' now. We're just ghosts to them."

The old man picked a long piece of cloth that had probably been a curtain some decades ago. He turned around to Ed and smiled.

"We call it 'Treasure Island'."

p.19

Ed blinked. His blurry mind figured out that he was somewhere on the northwest side of town, near the old mines. The area had been busy during the twenties and thirties because of the mining business. The barber from the shop next to Pie Heaven had told him that there used to be a beautiful old cinema here.

"Folks around here call me Willy. Professor Willy. Because I'm the only one who can read," the old man said.

He handed Ed the long piece of cloth. Ed took it reluctantly and wrapped it around himself. It smelled bad.

"I... I'm Ed," he managed to say.

The light of the moon played with the shadows. It was as if the street was alive.

"Nice to meet you, Ed. Now follow me," Willy said, and started down the street.

Ed followed Willy slowly, walking deeper into the darkness of the street.

진한 갈색과 연한 갈색이 반반 정도이지요? 시험 삼아 진한 갈색 부분만을 따로 떼어내어 읽어봅시다.

"Son, you're gonna freeze to death if you sleep here,"
"Son, you really better wake up."
An old man was standing over him.
"Son, I don't know what the heck you're doing here, but you better

wake up if you don't wanna become a damn Popsicle."

"Where am I?"

"You don't know where you are?"

"I think... I... I'm lost..."

"Damn right you are. Everyone who comes here is lost. Pretty badly lost, as a matter of fact."

The old man walked over to a giant pile of junk by the side of the road.

"People have forgotten about this place. They call it 'Ghost Avenue' now. We're just ghosts to them."

The old man picked a long piece of cloth

"We call it 'Treasure Island'."

"Folks around here call me Willy. Professor Willy. Because I'm the only one who can read,"

He handed Ed the long piece of cloth. Ed took it reluctantly and wrapped it around himself.

"I... I'm Ed,"

"Nice to meet you, Ed. Now follow me,"

Ed followed Willy slowly,

무척 간단한 문장이 되어버리지만, 내용만 이해하려고 한다면 이것으로도 충분해요. 본문의 각본 버전이라고 할 수 있지요.

그러나 이 문장들만으로는 지루하니까 실제 본문에서는 연한 갈색 부분을 덧붙였어요. 전부를 다 읽을 수 있다면 더할 나위가 없겠지만, 만약 너무 어려운 문장과 마주치면 진한 갈색 문장을 이야기의 주축으로 보고 읽어나가세요. 그리고 군데군데 나오는 연한 갈색 문장의 의미를 놓치지 말고 머릿속에서 분위기도 즐길 수 있다면 그것으로 충분해요.

pp.20-21

Meanwhile, in another part of town...
And back in Ghost Avenue...

우리말에도 이야기에서만 쓰이는 어휘가 상당히 있어요. '그 당시', '한편', '행복하게 살았습니다' 등등……. 이런 전환 어구는 일상 회화에서는 거의 사용하지 않아요. 이야기에서만 즐겨 쓰이는 표현이지요. 영어에도 이야기에서만 쓰이는 표현이 꽤 있어요. 위의 두 문장도 장면이 바뀔 때 쓰이는 전환 어구의 전형적인 예지요.

이처럼 이야기에서만 쓰이는 표현을 한번 익혀두면, 이야기의 흐름을 놓쳤을 때 도움이 됩니다. 특히 그림책과 아동 문학 작품에서는 자주 볼 수 있으므로 책에서 볼 때마다 뉘앙스를 살펴보세요.

이야기에서 자주 보이는 전환 어구

Elsewhere
(A에서 B로 무대가 이동할 때 사용해요)
Meanwhile
(A에서 B로 무대가 이동하고 동시에 일어난 사건을 보여줄 때 사용해요)
In another time
(SF나 판타지의 도입 부분에서 환상의 세계가 펼쳐지기 시작할 때 사용해요)
Far, far away
(역시 SF나 판타지의 도입 부분에서 사용해요. 우주의 저편을 떠올리게 하는 이미지)
Once upon a time
(우리말로 '옛날에'에 해당하는 표현. 전래 동화의 서두에 나오는 상용 문구)

Ingredients

(for the crust)	(for the filling)	
150g graham crackers	400g frozen pumpkin	1/4 teaspoon salt
2 tablespoons soft brown sugar	1/2 cup soft brown sugar	1 teaspoon cinnamon
1/3 cup melted butter or	2 tablespoons granulated sugar	1/4 teaspoon ginger
margarine	2 eggs	1/4 teaspoon nutmeg
	1/2 cup milk	1/4 teaspoon clove

A long time ago
(역시 옛날이야기의 서두에서 사용해요. Once upon a time보다 한층 현실적)
happily ever after
(전래 동화를 끝맺는 상용 문구. 우리말로는 '그 후로도 오랫동안 행복하게 살았습니다')
In the end
(최종 결론을 내릴 때 쓰는 관용어)
And back(in/to)
(TV에서 뉴스 스튜디오로 마이크가 넘어올 때 쓰는 표현)

Ghost Avenue는 어떤 '거리'?

그럼 본문으로 돌아가서 에드가 다다른 Ghost Avenue란 곳에 대해서 살짝 살펴봅시다. 물론 이 명칭은 정식 이름이 아니라 퇴락한 거리의 풍경 때문에 붙여진 속칭이에요. ghost는 일반적으로 '유령'을 일컫지만, 넓은 의미로는 '잔상'이란 애매한 의미도 있어요.

avenue는 '거리'를 가리키는 단어지만, 우리에게 친근한 단어는 street겠지요. street와 avenue의 차이는 미묘해요. 따져보자면, street가 일반적인 '거리'를 가리키는 데 비해 avenue는 비교적 큰 대로를 가리켜요. 그리고 street나 avenue는 번화가의 도로라는 인상이 강해요. 시골의 도로는 대개 road란 단어를 쓰지요. 한층 더 좁은 두렁길은 path라고 하고요.

글로만 설명해서는 이해가 잘 안 될 것 같아 각각의 이미지를 일러스트로 표현해보았습니다.

1.Crush the graham crackers into crumbs. Mix the soft brown sugar and melted butter into the crackers and mix well. Spread in pie dish. Press mixture with fingers until thin to form the piecrust.

path　　　road　　　street　　　avenue

미국의 시골 마을 중에는 Ghost Avenue처럼 한때 번화가였지만 시대에 뒤처져 폐허로 변해버린 곳이 자주 보여요. 우리나라는 토지 면적이 넓지 않아 바로 철거에 들어가지만 미국은 차라리 새로운 지역을 개발하는 것이 철거하는 것보다 비용이 덜 들거든요. 이처럼 버려진 마을은 차차 오갈 데 없는 사람들의 터전이 되어 결국 치안이 열악한 슬럼가가 된답니다.

30년 전쯤의 어느 날 시간이 멈추어버린 듯한 이런 마을은 실로 묘한 분위기가 있습니다. 먼 옛날에 사라진 상품을 '신상품'이라고 소개하는 포스터가 벽에 붙어 있는가 하면 여기저기 진열장에는 두 세대 전의 인기 상품이 먼지를 뒤집어쓴 채 있지요. 밝은 낮에도 사람의 그림자 하나 보이지 않고 세상이 멸망한 듯한 적막함이 일대를 가득 메우고 있어서 형언할 수 없는 상념에 젖게 해요.

윌리와 나누는 일상 회화

옛 에버빌 극장으로 무대가 이동하면서 이야기도 점차 후반으로 접어들고 있네요. 여기서부터는 에드와 윌리의 대화에 주목하면서 읽어봅시다. 〈Big Fat Cat and the Ghost Avenue〉에 나오는 대화는 지금까지 다루어온 앞 권들보다 현실에 더 가까워요. 따라서 격의

2.Remove the green skin from the frozen pumpkin after defrosting. Mash and strain pumpkin into puree form. Add rest of the ingredients for the filling and mix well.

없는 표현이나 이해하기 어려운 표현도 나온답니다. 의미를 잘 모른다고 해서 영어 실력이 부족하기 때문이라고 단정 짓지는 마세요. 회화의 의미를 이해하지 못하는 이유는 대부분 영어를 이해하지 못해서가 아니랍니다. 예를 들어 미국의 전형적인 젊은이들이 약속을 주고받는 경우를 생각해볼까요? 교과서에 실린 회화는 아마 아래와 같을 거예요.

"Please promise me you will come tomorrow."
"Sure, I promise."

하지만 이런 회화를 실제로 들을 수 있는 경우는 영어 회화 교실뿐이에요. 적어도 아래와 같이 축약하고 생략해서 표현하는 것이 일반적이랍니다.

"Promise me you'll come tomorrow."
"Sure."

그리고 친한 친구 사이라면 아래와 같은 회화문이 되겠지요.

"Tomorrow. Word?"
"Word."

이런 문장이 나왔을 때 이해를 못하는 것은 영어 실력 문제가 아니에요. word라는 단어를 아무리 사전에서 찾아보아도 이 대화에서 쓰인 의미는 전혀 알 수 없을 거예요. 그러나 실제로 이 어휘를 쓰고 있는 사람과 이야기를 하면서 그 당시의 상황과 표정이나 몸짓을 본다면 어떤 의미인지 알 수 있지요.
지방, 연령, 성별 등에 따라서 언어는 재미있게 변해요. 학교에서 가장 중시하는 문법도 회화 앞에서는 꼼짝 못하지요. 회화에서는 의사소통과 재미가 중요해요. 의사소통과 재미야말로 커뮤니케이션의 핵심 목표지요. 각양각색 사람들을 접하면서 말버릇과 어휘를 흡수하고,

3.Preheat oven to 200°C. Pour filling into piecrust and bake 45 minutes. (**CAUTION :** The piecrust can burn easily. Wrap the crust edges in foil if necessary.) Cool in refrigerator. Serve with whipped cream.

재미있다고 느낀 표현은 따라 하고 지루한 표현은 스쳐버리면서 점차 자신의 영어가 완성되어간답니다. 어느 누구의 모방이 아닌 자신만의 '영어'가 되는 것이지요. 그때를 목표로 차차 회화에 대한 경험을 쌓아가길 바랍니다. 군이 외국에 갈 필요는 없어요. 소설도 영화도 회화의 보고니까요. 우선 에버빌에 나오는 등장인물들과 회화를 즐겨보세요.

그럼 윌리의 대사로 초점을 좁혀서 살펴봅시다. 윌리는 에드에 비해 특징이 뚜렷한 말투이므로 당황한 분들도 있었을 거예요. 여기서 등장한 윌리의 대화를 아래에 정리해보았습니다.

> **줄임 표현들**
> gonna(p.14)는 going to,
> wanna(p.15)는 want to를 각
> 각 줄인 형태.
> 발음이 빨라서 소리가 축약된
> 채 들려요.

> **강조 표현들**
> 윌리가 에드를 son(p.14)이라고 부르
> 지만, 물론 실제 아들은 아니에요.
> 연배가 높은 사람이 자신보다 젊은
> 남성을 친근감 있게 부를 때 이렇게
> 부르기도 해요.
> Popsicle(p.15)은 그림과
> 같은 모양의 대중적인
> 아이스캔디.

> **강조 표현들**
> the heck, damn(p.15) 등은
> 특별히 깊은 의미는 없고 강조
> 하고자 쓴 단어.

p.22

"Here we are," Willy said, stopping in front of a unique two-story structure. Ed looked up at the building in wonder. It was a great big building.

The Old Everville Cinema really was beautiful. The barber had not been kidding. He had not been kidding about the 'old' part either. But the cinema still remained beautiful in a strange sort of way.

"This used to be a great theater back in the fifties, you know. Big screen, great flicks, buttered popcorn... But that was a long time ago.

Now it's our home," Willy said as he pushed open the doors of the once-glamorous theater.

실제 영어 회화에서 가장 자주 나오는 표현은 무엇일까요? and도 that도 아닙니다. 어떤 말버릇이에요. 이 페이지의 윌리 대사에 나오는 'you know'와 같은 관용구가 바로 말버릇이지요. 직역하면 '너도 알다시피'란 의미지만, 단독으로 회화문과 회화문 사이에 쓸 때는 별 뜻이 없어요. you know는 말이 막혔을 때 대부분의 미국인이 입에 담는 관용구랍니다. 영화배우의 인터뷰 등을 잘 들어보면 불쑥불쑥 나오는 것을 알 수 있어요. 긴장하면 사용빈도가 늘어나므로 상대의 기분을 관찰하는 하나의 기준이 되기도 하지요.

긴장하지 않은 에드
   "I think my blueberry pie is really delicious and I'm proud to have made it.

매우 긴장한 에드
   Uh... you know... I think my blueberry pie is... you know, really delicious, and... umm... I'm... you know, proud to have made it.

배경 묘사는 막연한 이미지만 그려도 충분해요

여기서는 영화관 내부의 모습을 설명하고자 해요. 그러나 이런 장면이 어려우면 무시해도 이야기 진행에 큰 영향은 없어요. 삽화를 참고하면 어떤 상황인지 바로 알 수 있겠지만, 삽화가 없는 책도 중요한 단어만 뽑아서 읽으면 머릿속에 대강의 모습이 그려지지요.

p.23

Inside, the theater lobby was ruined. The refreshment stand, the ticket booth, and the waiting area had been torn down, and everything had been replaced with piles of cardboard and miscellaneous junk. A few people were sitting there in the dark. The only light inside was a lantern hung from the remains of a chandelier.

A man rummaging through a pile of soda cans looked up and grinned at Ed.

"That's Frank," Willy said as he pushed his stroller through the mess. "He won't hurt you. Nice guy. Stinks, but a nice guy anyway."

"Howdy," Frank said to Ed, raising his hand awkwardly. He had no teeth. Ed just kept walking.

이 장면에서 최소한 파악해야 할 것은 'ruined', 'torn down(부서졌다)', 'dark' 등과 같은 전체적인 인상과 'cardboard(골판지)', 'junk(쓰레기)'와 같은 소도구로 그려지는 이미지입니다. 이런 단어가 주는 이미지를 빈 방에 채워 넣으면 이런 느낌이 아닐까요?

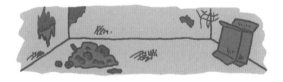

이 정도만 알 수 있다면 스토리를 읽기 위해서 필요한 무대 이미지로는 충분해요.
그 뒤로 다음 장면에서는 영화관 중심 쪽으로 옮겨가서 중심 부분의 무대 설정이 나와요.

p.24
   Willy walked across the lobby to a set of swinging doors that were
hidden behind a broken vending machine. Ed followed cautiously,
glancing around the whole time.
   **The main part of the theater was better preserved than the lobby,
except for one major difference. There was a big hole in the ceiling.** The
blue half moon shined through the hole, providing a soft light. There was
also a warm red glow from a small campfire that was burning directly
underneath the hole.

앞부분은 로비 주변의 모습을 그렸어요. 한 번 더 이미지를 떠올려봅시다. 전체적으
로는 'lobby(로비)', 자잘한 소도구로는 'swinging doors(여닫이문)', 'broken vending
machine(부서진 자동판매기)' 등이 있어요. 앞의 낡은 방에 소도구들을 둔다고 상상하면 아
마 이런 느낌이 될 거예요.

   미스터리 소설에서 밀실 살인을 묘사하는 경우가 아니라면, 무대 묘사는 대부분 '간격'을 두
기 위해 삽입되므로 이런 부분에서 사전을 찾거나 생각에 빠지면 무대 묘사의 가장 중요한 역
할인 '이야기 흐름의 조절'을 오히려 놓치게 돼요. 사전을 보는 건 결코 잘못된 것은 아니에요.
그러나 사전을 보다가 전체적인 흐름을 놓쳐버린다면 의미가 없어요.
   무대 설정은 막연한 이미지로도 충분해요. 혹시 이해가 안 가는 부분이 있다면 그 부분은 상
상으로 메워도 상관없어요. 상상이야말로 영상이 없는 매체인 소설 읽기의 묘미니까요.

이야기의 완급 즐기기

문장이 길게 이어지는 장면이 나오면 읽는 도중에 피곤해지는 경우가 있어요. 하지만 문장이 길면 길수록 중요한 부분과 '간격' 부분을 확실히 알 수 있지요. '간격' 부분은 음악의 간주와도 같아요. 이번 작품에서 가장 길기도 하고, 또 이야기의 중심이 되는 장면을 따라가면서 문장의 완급에 대해 살펴봅시다. 에드와 윌리가 장작불 부근에서 대화를 주고받는 장면이에요.

p.26

"Here. Use them."
Willy pointed to a row of seats near the campfire. Ed sat down. He found the seats very mushy, but he didn't care. The seats were much better than the cold street outside.
"Well, you've met Frank, and that's George and Beejees. Louie's in that box over there, I don't know where Paddy is, but Marv's probably in the basement. He almost never comes out."
Ed nodded.

처음 부분은 전부 연한 갈색이에요. 대화도 삽입되어 있지만, 여기서는 아직 도입부에 지나지 않기 때문에 가볍게 스치듯 읽어나가도 상관없어요.

p.27

"**What do you do for a living, Ed?**" Willy asked as he tossed a few crumpled-up pieces of newspaper into the fire.
"**I bake... I used to bake pies,**" Ed said, staring into the burning fire.

BEDTIME STORIES
from the Astyore Library

The Match Prince

"That's a nice job."

"I lost my shop yesterday. I'm not a baker anymore."

"Sure you are. You're just a baker without a shop."

p.28

"Not just my shop. I lost my house, my savings, my bag, my whole life... all I have left is this."

Ed took his rolling pin out of his coat pocket. Somebody had found it lying near him in the parking lot of the New Mall. It always seemed to survive somehow. Ed tossed it on the ground.

It rolled straight toward the fire. It would have burned up if Willy hadn't reached out and grabbed it.

"Don't. This is important to you."

"No," Ed said. "I'm really not much of a baker. I just like baking pies. I was a mediocre salesman until last year. I quit my job, thinking I could become a pie baker because my mom used to bake great pies. She won a lot of contests. I thought maybe I was like her. But I wasn't. Stupid."

적게나마 '간격'이 되는 연한 갈색 문장이 군데군데 섞여 있지만 중요한 대화가 이어집니다. 에드도 윌리도 거의 동작이 없으므로 기본적으로 가장 중요한 것은 대화 부분이지요. 대화가 많이 나오는 장면은 전체 이야기에서 중요한 부분이 되는 경우가 많아요. 대화 중심으로 제대로 읽어주세요.

Willy stood by the fire, listening with a faint smile on his face. It was a smile worn by time and hardened, almost petrified, by the burdens of life.

The Match Prince

(1) nce upon a time, there was a land of matches. The match people lived there. Water was more valuable than money in the Match Kingdom, because their heads would ignite easily. If they became angry, their heads got hot and burst into fire. If they caught a cold and developed a fever, their heads would heat up and burst into fire. So water was always kept near.

1

ignite 불타다 | burst into fire 갑자기 불이 붙다 | cold 감기 | develop 발전하다 | fever 열

Ed continued to speak, the light of the fire playing on his face.

"Mom always told me that life was like a blueberry pie. Sometimes it's sour but most of the time it's sweet. She said the most wonderful thing in life was to eat a good, warm slice of pie."

A tear formed at the corner of Ed's eye and rolled down his cheek.

p.31

"But she was wrong, you know. She died of a heart attack when I was in high school. From overwork. My father had left us the year before, and she'd had to work two jobs to raise me. One day when I came home from school, there was a slice of warm blueberry pie on the table. She was sitting in front of the oven, waiting for the pie to cool. But... she wasn't breathing. No last words. I never even said 'thank you' to her. I was too late. I'm always too damn late."

에드의 이야기가 핵심에 가까워질수록 대화문이 길어지고 중요도가 올라갑니다. 연한 갈색 문장은 점점 줄어들고…… 마침내 사라져가요.

Willy walked up to Ed and held the rolling pin out to him. Ed shook his head, tears streaming down his face.

"No. I'm not going to bake any more pies. Life isn't a blueberry pie. A child can see that. It's... it's... more like a mustard pie."

"Look, Ed. You're going to get a good night's sleep, and then in the morning, you're going to go back to your life. You are not one of us. You have a life. Go back to it."

"You don't understand. I can't bake pies like my mother. I don't have it

---

The Match Prince

There was a big lake in the Match Kingdom so water was always plenty. But things changed. The good king Matchionne died of the flu, and Karl Matches became the next king. Karl Matches was a greedy match. He built a watergate around the lake and decided to sell water at a high rate. Soon, the river in the Match Kingdom stopped flowing.

2

flu 독감 greedy 탐욕스러운 rate 가격 flow or flowing 흐르는 것

in me. I was only pretending I could."

"That's because you have no idea what a pie is really made of."

"Sure I do. I use the same things my mother did. I even use the same brand of flour. It doesn't make any difference."

"You had a great mom. She understood life well. She knew why pies were important. That's why she was a great baker."

"Pies are just pies. They're not important."

대화가 핵심에 들어서자 연한 갈색 문장은 전부 사라져버렸어요. 중요한 장면은 천천히 읽는 것도 좋지만 이야기의 속도를 잃지 않는 것 역시 중요해요. 읽는 속도는 사람마다 다르므로 자신이 질리지 않을 정도의 속도를 정해서 읽으면 그것이 최선입니다. 읽는 도중에 이해가 되지 않아서 힘들다면 너무 꼼꼼하게 읽고 있는 것인지도 몰라요. 설사 영어라 해도 책을 읽을 때는 어디까지나 '이야기를 읽는' 것이 최대의 목적입니다. '영어'를 읽으려고 들면 이야기가 머리에 들어오지도 않고 재미도 없어요. 단어나 표현을 보고 암기하는 데 급급하다가 글의 분위기나 뉘앙스를 놓쳐버리면 읽은 후에도 기억에 남지를 않고요. 하지만 이야기를 즐기면서 읽으면 영어는 자연히 머리에 들어온답니다. 그리고 이야기와 함께 언제까지나 기억에 남지요.

pp.32-33

A long silent moment passed. Ed looked away while Willy tended the fire. The crackling sounds of the fire eating into the wood filled the air. Finally, Willy spoke. His voice was slow and calm.

"Most of us haven't had a slice of pie in years, Ed."

Ed stopped wiping his tears. Still wearing that faint and petrified smile, Willy continued, "Take Frank for example. He's been here for more than ten years now. He's probably forgotten what a pie looks like."

The Match Prince

Young prince, Karl Matches the 2nd, who sometimes secretly went to the city, was not like his father. He was a good match who loved his kingdom. He tried to persuade his father, but King Matches wouldn't listen. Meanwhile, a bad flu was growing in the city and all the match children began to get hot heads. They were going to burst into fire at any time.

3

---

secretly 비밀스럽게 persuade 설득하다

Willy gestured toward Frank, who was now near the campfire, looking for something in another big pile of junk.

한참 떠들던 에드의 말이 끝나자 한동안 침묵이 주변을 감쌉니다. 타닥타닥 불타오르면서 흩어지는 불꽃 소리가 대화 사이의 침묵을 부각시키는 역할을 하고요. 이런 문장도 자세히 이 해할 필요는 없어요. 세세한 문법보다는 분위기를 느끼는 것이 훨씬 중요하니까요.

예를 들어 세 번째 문장에서 장작불의 모습을 묘사하고 있는데, 'fire가 wood를 eating하 고 있다'라고 표현했어요. 조금 기묘하게 비칠지도 모르지만 분위기가 있는 표현이지요. 이런 색다른 표현은 장면과 분위기와 함께 암기해주세요. 어떤 분위기에서 쓰이는 표현인지 익힐 수 있다는 것이 이야기를 통해서 영어를 배울 때의 큰 장점입니다. 단순한 예문만으로는 분위 기까지 알 수가 없으니까요.

pp.33-34

"Why doesn't he just buy one?" Ed said with a rather guilty look on his face. "I mean, he could get a job, couldn't he? A pie is just a buck or so. Frank chose to be here... just like me. Bad luck, but it's probably his own fault. Anybody can buy a piece of pie. You just need to go out and..."

At that moment, Frank moved toward the fire. Ed suddenly noticed that he had no legs.

The tears came back all at once. Ed's face turned red and he covered his mouth with his hand. The tears streamed over his hand.

"I'm... I'm sorry. I didn't mean... oh no... I'm... I'm so sorry. I'm so confused... I'm really, really sorry..."

"No harm done, Ed," Willy said. "Frank was born on the street. Never knew his parents... A car hit him when he was twenty. Three hospitals

---

The Match Prince

Prince Karl knew he had to destroy the watergate. But the watergate was guarded by many soldier matches and he would never be able to bring a weapon near it. He needed something to destroy the gate. But how? The children were almost on fire. Mothers were crying in despair. Prince Karl knew there was only one way. He went to the watergate. The guards let him in after they checked for weapons. They found none.

4

guarded 방어를 받다 soldier 병사 weapon 무기 despair 절망

refused to treat him and he ended up here."

대화문도 그렇습니다. 이번 작품까지 에드를 따라온 분이라면 모두 에드의 성격을 잘 알고 있을 거예요. 이는 매우 중요합니다. 우리말만큼은 아니더라도 영어도 사람에 따라 말투에 차이가 있어요. 굳은 표정의 프로레슬러가 '그치? 예쁘지'와 같은 말투를 쓴다면 어색하겠지요? (재미있을지도 모르겠지만.) 역시 '그렇군. 최고야'와 같은 조금은 거친 말투가 자연스러워요. Big Fat Cat의 캐릭터는 일부러 타입별로 전형적인 말투를 사용하도록 했답니다. 에드는 심약하고 친절하고, 제레미는 다소 거만한 말투에, 윌리는 온화한 노인의 말투로요.

pp.34-35

The soft light of the moon enveloped the theater in its warm glow. The smoke from the campfire rose through the hole in the ceiling, up toward the sky, where it scattered among the clouds. The whole theater seemed like a gentle shelter for life.

"Ed... most of us here will die without eating another piece of pie... and we're the luckier ones. Some people never have the chance to eat pie. Not once in their lives. Some people have never had anything sweet, not in their mouths or in their hearts. For those people, Ed, life isn't a blueberry pie or a mustard pie. Life is just hell."

Willy put the rolling pin down on the seat beside Ed and turned toward the campfire again.

"Sleep, Ed. Then go back. Bake more pies."

장면의 속도가 종반으로 갈수록 안정되어감에 따라, 점차 연한 갈색 문장이 늘어갑니다. 읽어갈 때도 긴장을 늦춥시다. 살짝 건너뛰어도 괜찮아요. 하지만 '블루베리 파이'나 '머스터드

The Match Prince

Prince Karl approached the gate. He thought about the suffering town. He thought about his selfish father. He was mad. He was really mad. Prince Karl raised his hands toward the castle and shouted "Father!!" and his head burst into flame. The fire caught on to the watergate and the gate broke open. The water attacked Karl Matches' castle by the lake and destroyed it. The matches were saved, but Prince Karl never returned.

The End

suffering 괴로워하다 selfish 이기적인

파이'가 나오거든, 즉 이야기의 키워드가 눈에 띄거든 그 문장만큼은 제대로 읽어주세요.

p.36

And it was a long night. The longest night of Ed's life. He was as tired as possible, but he still could not sleep.

He watched the campfire burn down.

He watched the moon shining in the sky.

And he watched the "ghosts" of Everville sleeping in their beds of garbage. Garbage that he might have thrown away.

He thought about all the pies he had baked. He thought even more about the many pies he had thrown away.

p.37

He thought of his mother.

He thought of his mother a lot that night.

Life is like a blueberry pie, Eddie. Sometimes it's sour, but most of the time, it's sweet.

For the first time in ten years, **Ed remembered that there was something after those words.** Perhaps the most important part which he had forgotten a long time ago.

And you know what, Eddie? It's always sweet if you eat it with the people you love.

Ed cried himself to sleep, and in the morning, he knew what he had to do.

영화라면 카메라가 에드로부터 점점 멀어지는 순간입니다. 이에 따라 연한 갈색 부분인 정경 묘사가 늘어나고 마지막 장면은 진한 갈색 문장으로 마무리 지었어요.

이탤릭체로 씌어진 문장은 매우 중요한 부분입니다. 이탤릭체로 씌어진 대화문이 나오면 그 부분은 캐릭터가 아주 큰 목소리로 말하고 있다고 생각하면서 읽어주세요. 마찬가지로 이탤릭체로 씌어진 내레이션이 나오면 그 부분은 마치 영화에서처럼, 웅숭깊은 소리 즉 에코 효과를 덧입힌 울리는 소리가 나온다고 상상하면서 읽어보세요.

하나의 장면에도 이처럼 중요한 부분과 그렇지 않은 부분이 섞여 있어요. 그 이유는 이야기가 전개되면서 시간이 경과하기 때문입니다. 두 대화문 사이에 살짝 '간격'을 두고 읽어주기를 작가가 바란다면, '잠시 침묵이 흘렀다'라고만 써서는 그 문장을 읽는 순간밖에 독자는 그곳에 머무르질 않아요. 이는 당연한 일이지요. 특히 시간이란 가장 상상하기 어려운 '개념'입니다. 그러므로 정경 묘사나 주변 이야기를 그림으로써 실제로 그 부분을 읽는 시간을 늘려서 물리적으로 읽는 속도를 늦추는 수밖에 없어요.

이런 '간격' 부분이 '중요하지 않다'라는 것은 사실 틀린 말입니다. 중요하지 않은 부분은 없어요. 그러나 더 중요한 부분은 있습니다.

책을 처음 읽을 때는 우선 전체의 의미를 파악하는 것을 목표로 읽어주세요. 세세한 부분은 스치고 지나가도 괜찮아요. 이렇게 읽는 편이 다시 읽을 때 즐거움도 늘어날 테니까요.

1. 보물찾기

이제 이야기도 종반으로 접어들었습니다. 스토리의 '원동력'이 되는 진한 갈색 문장과 '간격'이 되는 연한 갈색 문장에 대해서 이제 충분히 설명했다고 생각합니다. 자세한 설명은 이 정도에서 멈추고 남은 장면에서는 마치 보물을 찾는 기분으로 영어의 재미있는 표현들을 찾아봅시다. 언뜻 평범해 보이는 문장에도 재미있는 뉘앙스가 담긴 단어나 표현이 숨어 있어요. 이를 찾는 것이 같은 책을 다시 읽을 때의 즐거움이 아닐까요.

pp.38-41

When Willy woke up that morning, he couldn't believe what he smelled. It was the smell of fresh-baked pie. It was something he hadn't smelled for a long, long time. Willy got up and found his fellow ghosts standing around the campfire with Ed.

Ed was slicing up an apple pie.

"I'll be darned," Willy mumbled, his eyes wide with astonishment.

A metal container was hanging over the campfire, and more pies were baking inside of it. Ed saw Willy and spoke to him with a smile.

"I only had enough money for apple jam, so I guess it's not a genuine apple pie. And the crust is just graham crackers. But I did the best I could. I saved you a big piece. Here."

Willy took the slice of apple pie from Ed. It was on a piece of wax paper. No fork, no napkin, but it was really apple pie.

"You were right. I guess I am a baker after all," Ed said.

"Would you like to buy a car?" Mark asked me at the cafeteria one afternoon. I had been looking for an inexpensive car since last year, so I immediately said "Sure." Mark continued. "I have a friend that wants to sell his car really cheap." "That's great." "There's one little problem." "What?" "His girlfriend died in the back seat."

1

inexpensive 비싸지 않은 cheap 싸게

Willy bit into the pie. It was sweet. It smelled of a long time ago.
"Thank you," Willy said with a big smile.

Ed smiled back and said, "I'm going to get some more wax paper."

"Sure. Oh, Paddy's probably out in front of the theater sweeping. Please give him a slice too."

"Okay, I'll look for him," Ed said, and stepped out of the theater.

우리나라에서는 보통 '애플파이'를 주문하면 1인분만큼 잘라서 나오지만, 미국에서는 거대한 애플파이가 통째로 나와요. 이 페이지를 잘 살펴보면 알겠지만 '파이 전체'를 표현할 때는 'an apple pie', '파이 한 조각'을 표현할 때는 'a slice of apple pie'라고 구체적으로 구분해서 쓰고 있어요.

영어에는 이처럼 'a 단위 of 사물'을 써서 '전체'와 '1인분'으로 구별하는 표현이 무척 많아요. 특히 음식과 관련된 표현이 풍부해요. a slice of apple pie, a cup of coffee 등과 같은 표현은 미국의 식문화에서 빠뜨릴 수 없을 만큼 많이 쓰이지요. 그러나 이는 어디까지나 정확한 표기를 한 경우이고 일상 회화에서는 별로 구분하지 않고 섞어서 써요. 익숙해질 때까지 크게 신경 쓰지는 마세요.

여기에 등장하는 단어 중 가장 재미있는 단어는 guess랍니다. 원래 이 화살표는 '(퀴즈의 답을) 추측하다'와 같은 의미로 쓰여요. 하지만 회화에서는 조금 다른 형태로 쓰이는 경우가 많습니다.

우리말 문장을 머릿속으로 생각한 다음 영어로 번역해서 쓰려면 이상하게도 'I think~'로 시작하는 문장이 많아져요. 그 이유는 '~라고 생각한다'라는 표현을 평소에 자주 사용하고 이를 직역하면 'I think~'가 되어버리기 때문이에요.

하지만 think는 엄밀히 말하면 '고안하다'에 해당하는 단어입니다. 머리를 싸매고 숙고한 결과를 나타내는 단어로, 우리말의 '~라고 생각한다'처럼 가벼운 느낌이 없어요. 매우 냉정한

"She died?" "Yeah. Suicide. She cut her wrist." "God..." "He changed the whole back seat so it's clean." "Then why sell it?" "Well... he said he saw something in the rearview mirror while he was driving." "What?" "He didn't tell me what he saw. He just wants to sell the car. He said even one grand would be OK. And it's a Mercedes." "One grand for a Mercedes!?"
2

suicide 자살 one grand 1,000달러 Mercedes 메르세데스 벤츠

울림이 있는 단어랍니다.

그렇다면 '(단순히, 즉흥적으로) ~라고 생각한다'라는 뉘앙스를 표현하려면 어떤 단어를 쓰는 게 좋을까요? 여기 나온 guess가 바로 그럴 때 사용할 수 있는 표현입니다. 물론 완전히 똑같다고는 할 수 없지만 'guess'에는 우리말의 '~라고 생각한다'와 같이 부드러운 뉘앙스가 있답니다.

2. 퍼즐 맞추기

p.42

> But Paddy wasn't there.
>
> Instead, **Ed saw a big black man standing by the side of Ghost Avenue. The man's eyes were searching for something.** Ed froze, the slice of apple pie held in his hand. He recognized the man from somewhere. **The man looked like the bodyguard who had been standing behind the rich man at the New Mall's office.** He also looked a lot like the man who had grabbed his bag.
>
> At that moment, the man's eyes met Ed's eyes, and Ed suddenly knew what the man had been searching for.
>
> Because the man had just found it.

에드가 제레미의 보디가드와 대치하는 이 부분은 이번 작품에서 가장 어려운 장면일 수도 있어요. 특히 위의 예문은 대역을 자주 이용한, 영어 특유의 표현이 많이 나와요. 이 장면을 대역 없이 다시 쓰면 아래와 같은 문장이 됩니다.

So I bought the car. At first, the story bothered me a little. While I was driving around, I kept looking into the rearview mirror all the time. But I never saw anything. Two months passed and I started to forget about the mirror. The car was great and I felt sorry for the previous owner. He was probably hallucinating after his lover's shocking death. A year passed, and then two years.

3

bothered 괴롭히다 previous 이전의 hallucinating 환각을 일으키다

Ed found a black man standing in front of the theater.

The black man was Jeremy's bodyguard.

He was looking for Ed.

The black man found Ed.

하지만 지금까지 Big Fat Cat 시리즈를 읽어온 분이라면 이제 이런 문장은 지루하다고 느낄 것입니다. 〈Big Fat Cat and the Ghost Avenue〉에서도 마지막 장면을 맞이해서 지금까지와는 다른 상당히 간접적인 표현을 선택했어요. 천천히 살펴봅시다.

우선 black man이 서 있는 장소를 확인해볼까요? 본문에서는 단순히 '영화관 앞'이라고 쓰지 않았어요. 앞 장면에서 '패디는 영화관 앞에 있다'라는 문장으로 끝을 맺었으므로 'But Paddy wasn't there(there=영화관 앞)'라는 문장으로 시작하여 자동적으로 에드가 영화관 앞에 와 있다는 사실을 전했어요.

이어서 black man이 에드를 찾고 있는 장면, 그리고 마침 에드를 찾은 장면은 아래의 세 문장에 걸쳐서 설명했어요.

The man's eyes were searching for something.

At that moment, the man's eyes met Ed's eyes, and Ed suddenly knew what the man had been searching for.

Because the man had just found it.

우선 black man이 눈으로 something을 찾고 있는데, 그 something이 무엇인지는 밝히지 않은 채 다음 문장에서 에드와 black man의 시선이 마주쳐요. 그리고 에드는 바로 black man이 찾고 있는 대상이 '무엇인지(what)' 눈치 채지요. 마지막 문장에서는 something이 it으로 되어 있지만, 역시 it이 무엇인지는 확실히 드러나지 않았어요. 이미 잘 알고 있겠지만 찾고 있던 something은 바로 지금 눈이 마주친 '에드'지요.

Seven years later, the car engine finally broke down and I decided to sell it. I had completely forgotten about the rearview mirror. I drove to a junkyard and parked the car one final time. I reached over to the passenger's seat to open the glove compartment and accidentally bumped my head into the rearview mirror. "Ouch." I said and looked up.

4

junkyard 고물을 모아두는 장소 glove compartment 글로브 박스(자동차 앞좌석 앞에 있는 장갑 등을 넣어두는 칸)
bumped 부딪치다

이는 실체가 분명히 드러나지 않는 막연한 '대상'이라도 얼마든지 다른 대역으로 바꾸어 표현할 수 있는, 영어 특유의 표현이랍니다. 'black man이 찾고 있는 것'이라는 애매모호한 대상을 something이나 what 혹은 it으로 바꾸어 표현한 것이지요. 이처럼 영어에선 퍼즐과 같은 문장을 많이 만들 수 있어요.

우리말에서 시종일관 '저것', '그것', '그'와 같은 대역을 사용하면 상대로부터 불평을 듣기 십상이에요. 그러나 영어에선 대역을 쓰는 것이 오히려 깔끔한 문장이 되므로 선호하는 경향이 있어요. 처음에는 까다롭게 느껴지겠지만 익숙해지면 퍼즐을 푸는 듯한 기분으로 즐길 수 있게 된답니다. 따라서 이런 표현이 나오거든 언어 유희를 한다는 느낌으로 도전해보길 바라요. 하지만 잘 이해가 가지 않을 때는 신경 쓰지 마세요. 본래의 의도 자체가 이해하기 어렵도록 한번 꼬아서 사용한 문자니까요.

3. 생략

p.43

Ed started to turn around, but it was too late. **The man seized Ed from behind and slammed him against the outside wall of the theater.**

"No words," the man whispered to Ed as he held him against the wall. Completely terrified, Ed was unable to speak anyway.

"Understand?" the man whispered again.

Ed nodded desperately, although he could not understand what was happening at all. He could barely breathe.

The giant black man stuffed a piece of paper in Ed's mouth and said just two more words.

"Sign it."

Ed nodded at once. It was the only thing he could do.

I screamed. The mirror had turned sideways. It was now reflecting a part of the back seat I never saw in the mirror until now. A woman covered in red was looking at me with sad, angry eyes. It had been there, lying in the small foot space behind the driver's seat, all these years, watching me in silence.

END

reflecting 반사하다

우리말은 생략하기 쉬운 언어입니다. 외국인을 대상으로 한 국어 교재를 펼쳐보지 않는 한, 어디서나 생략된 문형을 볼 수 있어요. 특히 일상 회화에서 생략은 뛰어난 함축 기능을 보여줘요. 예를 들어 '내일 저와 함께 영화 보러 가지 않을래요?'라는 의미를 전달하고 싶을 때 우리말로는 '내일 영화 볼래?'라고 간단히 말할 수 있지요. 마음이 통하는 친구끼리는 그저 '이거 갈래?'라는 말로도 충분히 의미가 전달되기도 해요.

이에 비해 영어는 우리말만큼 간단히 생략할 수 없어요. 하지만 전혀 생략할 수 없는 것은 아니에요. 위의 예문에서 black man은 최소한의 단어만을 사용하여 자신의 의사를 표현해요. 그러나 영어에선 A 상자의 주인공을 생략하면 자동적으로 '명령문'이 되므로 생략하면 할수록 고압적이고 자칫 무례한 표현이 되어버린답니다. 게다가 '약속하다'를 'Word'라는 한 단어로 바꿔 표현한 것처럼 슬랭이 생략의 주된 형태지요. 단, 슬랭은 시대와 함께 변화하므로 자연스럽게 입에 붙을 때까지는 그리 권하고 싶지는 않아요.

4. 절묘한 결합

p.44

The man let him go. Ed dropped to his knees on the ground, the pie falling from his hand. The man tossed a pen at Ed, and then started walking back to the limousine. Shaking all over, Ed picked up the pen and started signing his name. He couldn't think. He was too scared.

Before he finished signing his name, the sound of the limousine door rang in his ear. Ed raised his eyes from the ground and saw something that made his blood run cold.

The man was holding Ed's bag.

And something was stuffed inside. Something very still.

Something shaped like a big, fat cat.

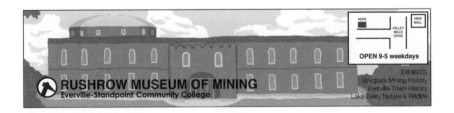

사람의 동작은 'jump', 'walk'와 같이 단순한 형태만 있지는 않아요. 특히 도저히 한 단어로는 표현이 불가능한 경우도 있어요. '잡아두었던 사람을 풀어주다', '다리가 풀려서 주저앉다'와 같은 동작을 행동으로 옮기기는 간단하지만, 한 단어로 표현하는 화살표는 없으므로 문장으로 표현할 때는 궁리를 해보아야 해요.

여기서는 이처럼 한 단어가 아닌 변형된 화살표를 소개하고자 합니다.

위의 예문에서 The man let him go가 실제로는 어떤 행동이었을까요? 벽으로 밀어붙여서 결박했던 에드를 '풀어주었다'란 의미입니다. let은 '어떤 행동을 허가하다'라는 의미를 지닌 살짝 변형된 화살표입니다. 여기서는 'him(에드)'이 'go'하는 행동을 black man이 허가했다는 뜻이에요. 다시 말해 '풀어주다'라는 의미가 되지요. let go를 무조건 '손에 쥔 것을 놓다/해방하다'란 뜻으로 외워버리면 실제 문장에서 어떤 의미로 쓰이는지 모르게 되므로 응용할 수가 없어요. 그러므로 이런 숙어는 반드시 각 문장에서 단어 단위로 잘라서 쓰임을 이해해야 합니다.

dropped to his knees는 온몸에서 힘이 빠져나가 균형을 잃어버린 것처럼 무릎이 꺾이는 모습을 나타내요. 여기서 dropped한 사람은 에드 '자신'이지요. Shaking all over의 all은 '전신'을 나타내고요. over는 '전체에 걸쳐서'란 부록으로 온몸이 부들부들 떨리는 모습을 가리켜요.

run cold 앞에 붙은 '배우'가 blood이므로 쉽게 이해했으리라고 생각하지만 굳이 우리말로 옮기면 '소름이 끼친' 느낌을 나타냅니다.

이처럼 사전상의 단어 의미만으로는 알 수 없는 인간의 감각과 감정을 어떻게 표현하는지 살펴보면 그 언어 문화의 특성을 알 수 있어요. 아무리 거리가 멀고 인종이 달라도 상황에 따른 비유가 비슷하다는 사실을 알게 되면 다른 나라의 사람과 언어에 대해서도 훨씬 친근감이 들 거예요.

5. 과장

pp.45-48

The man came back, and set the bag down in front of Ed. Then the man picked up the paper. He checked the signature quickly, and without even a glance at Ed, started back to the limousine.

Ed's heart was bouncing in his chest. He had the urge to throw up but he pushed it back. He remembered thinking that all of his problems were the cat's fault.

"Oh, cat... I'm sorry... I'm so sorry..."

Ed slowly pulled the zipper of the bag open.

"AAAGGGGGHHHHHH!!"

Ed shouted as a very frustrated cat popped out of the bag with a snarl and scratched his face. The cat leaped aside, and almost immediately noticed the piece of pie on the ground. The cat took a giant stretch, and with the grace that only cats possess, approached the pie and started to devour it.

A smile of relief appeared on Ed's face, as he sat down on the sidewalk weakly. The limousine had already driven away. Ed leaned against the wall of the theater and let out a deep breath. He still couldn't understand what that had been all about. It was probably something about the vacant space in the mall, but he didn't care anymore. He was just glad that it was over.

The cat finished the piece of pie and looked up at Ed for more. It seemed dissatisfied, maybe because the pie was not blueberry.

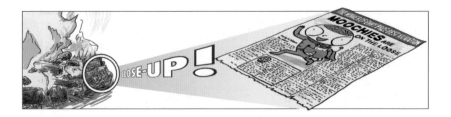

"You understand a lot more than you seem to, don't you, cat?" Ed asked. A weak but sincere smile spread across his face.

"Blueberry pie is the only pie I still make from my mom's original recipe."

Ed looked into the cat's eyes. The cat looked back. <u>It was a weird but pleasant moment, there on the sidewalk of a forgotten town. One cat and its owner, just staring at each other awkwardly.</u>

Then, after a long silent moment, the cat burped.

영어와 우리말의 가장 큰 차이는 무엇일까요? 물론 언어의 구조도 다르고 단어의 쓰임도 다르고 이외에도 여러 차이들이 있지만 개중에서도 영어는 '과장'이 심하다고 할 수 있어요. 영어를 쓰면서 재미있게 느낀 점 중의 하나는, 바로 우리말로는 부끄러워서 하지 못했던 말들을 영어로는 부담 없이 쓸 수 있다는 사실입니다. 민족성의 차이 때문인지, 영어가 그다지 감정을 담아내는 언어가 아니기 때문인지는 확실하지 않지만 우리말로 표현할 때는 거창하게 들리는 '너를 사랑한다'는 말도 영어로 'I love you'라고 하면 매우 일상적인 표현이 된다는 점이 신기해요. 위의 밑줄 그은 부분은 영어다운 오버액션과 과장이 있는 부분이에요. 다시 읽을 때는 반드시 이런 '영어다운' 부분을 즐기길 바랍니다.

6. 최후의 도전

p.49

"Ugh! That's horrible," Ed laughed.

The cat made an annoyed face, and started to look for somewhere warm to take a nap. It still seemed hungry. Ed's laughter echoed down the wide, empty road of Ghost Avenue, up and down, over and below, and on into the

Jeremy Lightfoot Jr.'s
Words of **Wisdom**

"There are only two kinds of people. Me, and everyone else."

Jeremy Lightfoot Jr.

first glimpse of the day ahead.

Ed Wishbone knew that the rest of his life had begun.

이 장면은 조금 어려운 문장으로 끝맺고 있어요. 마지막에서 두 번째 문장은 3색사전에 나오는 색깔 구분을 보면 잘 알 수 있겠지만, 사실은 무척 단순한 문장이에요. 80퍼센트가 여러 '장소'를 나타내는 부록인 셈이지요. (정확히 말하면 '시간'과 '장소'가 다 있는 부록) 끝맺는 문장은 에드가 이날을 지금까지의 인생과 남은 인생의 분기점으로 삼으려 한다는 사실을 상기하면서 읽으면 이해하기 쉬울 것입니다.

7. 뉘앙스 찾기

어떤 문장이든 전후 관계가 있어요. 그 문장이 등장하는 배경이 있고요. 언제, 어디서, 누가 무엇 때문에 이 문장을 썼을까. 이런 배경에 대한 이해가 내용을 이해하는 것보다 더 중요할 수도 있답니다. 문법이라는 규칙을 만들어서 끈질기게 문장을 이해하려고 하는 이유도 바로 문장에 포함된 세세한 뉘앙스까지도 놓치지 않기 위해서가 아닐까요?

해설의 83~92쪽에서는 문장에 숨어 있는 여러 가지 뉘앙스에 대해 설명했어요. 그러니 이 이야기를 두 번 이상 읽을 때부터는 반드시 이런 세세한 뉘앙스까지도 파악해가면서 '어?' 하고 의아한 부분이 있거든 골똘히 생각해보세요.

그리고 한 문장 한 문장 영어에 숨어 있는 뉘앙스를 정리해서 머릿속에 보관하세요. 시간은 걸릴지 몰라도 이는 보물찾기와도 같답니다. 숨겨진 뉘앙스를 발견할 때마다 마음의 영어 상자를 열어 보물을 채워 넣다 보면, 상자의 바닥이 보이지 않게 될 즈음에는 영어 상자 자체가 보물로 바뀌어 있을 것입니다.

사소한 단어나 문법은 버리자. 이야기의 세계에 마음을 맡기자

이번 해설에서는 1, 2권과는 달리 대화문, 속도, 간격, 중요도라는 관점에서 이야기를 살펴보았습니다. 모든 문장을 색으로 구분했지만 이는 중요도를 파악하기 위한 하나의 방법에 불과해요. 연한 글씨가 얼마나 있는지 실제로 보여주기 위해 색 구분을 한 것이지. 즉 '이렇게 건너뛰고 읽어도 이야기의 의미를 파악할 수 있다'라는 한마디를 전하기 위해서 이 해설이 있다고 해도 과언이 아닙니다.

책을 좋아하는 분들일수록 '건너뛰고 읽기'에 저항을 느낄 수도 있을 거예요. 그러나 책을 좋아하기 때문에 건너뛰고 읽어서라도 읽고 싶은 것이라고 생각해본다면 어떨까요?

어린 시절, 읽지 못하는 책이라도 어쩐지 읽고 싶은 마음에 그림을 보며 상상의 나래를 펴고 이야기를 짜 맞추던 경험이 있지 않은가요? 아무리 잘못 이해하고, 아무리 건너뛰고 읽어도 좋은 책은 신기하게도 재미가 전달된답니다. 처음부터 끝까지 구석구석 제대로 이해가 될 때까지 몇 번이나 반복해서 읽게 하는 힘이 있어요. 하지만 읽기가 안 되는 사소한 이유가 있다고 해서 읽지 않게 되면 영원히 그 이야기와는 만날 수 없잖아요. 이런 경우야말로 가장 안타까운 상황이지요.

책을 펼치거든 이야기의 세계에 몸과 마음을 맡기세요. 이야기를 즐기다 보면 문득문득 영어가 조금씩 이해되기 시작할 것입니다.

피가 통하지 않는 단순한 예문들보다는 숨결을 불어넣은 캐릭터들을 믿으세요. 에드도 고양이도 언제나 이야기 저편에서 기다리고 있으니까요!

Big Fat Cat의 디저트

이번 디저트는 상당히 가치가 있는 자료랍니다.
고스트 애비뉴가 번화가였을 당시,
영화관 재오픈에 맞추어 배부되었던 광고 전단지가
러시로 광산 박물관에 보관되어 있습니다.

이번에는 그 광고가 실린
박물관 팸플릿의 한 페이지를 보여드릴게요.

지금은 폐허가 되어버린 고스트 애비뉴의
지난날의 모습이 전단지에는 오롯이 남아 있습니다.
현재의 모습과 비교해보면서 색다른 재미를 즐겨보세요.

Grand Opening Flier, 1962

⊕ RUSHROW MUSEUM OF MINING

THE "PALACE" YEARS (1928-1960)

During the "Gold Rush" of Spyglass Mountains, "The Palace" started out as a multi-purpose theater for the workers and families in the surrounding area. It quickly became the center of entertainment and enjoyed more than thirty years of good business.

THE "NEW PALACE" YEARS (1928-1960)

After the damage of the 1960 hurricane, the Palace changed ownership and went under complete renovation. The New Palace was designed for a much tounger and pop-cultural audience but failed after only seventeen months. The main reason was the high rise ticket prices.

THE "EVERVILLE CINEMA" YEARS (1962-1979)

After yet another change in ownership, the New Palace became "Everville Cinema" and survived another decade as a family theater for second-run movies. The theater finally ended its long history in the fall of 1979. Currently, the city of Everville plans to revive the theater as a historical landmark, but the project is still in its early stage of development.

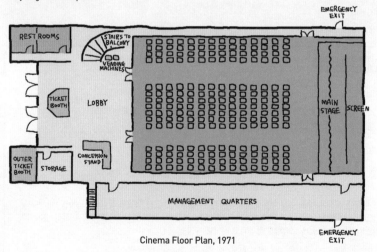

Cinema Floor Plan, 1971

BIG FAT CAT'S
3 COLOR
DICTI⬤NARY

BIG FAT CAT
and the
GHOST AVENUE

빅팻캣의 3색사전
~고스트 애비뉴 편~

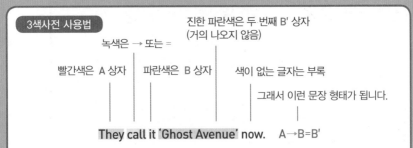

3색사전 사용법

진한 파란색은 두 번째 B′ 상자
(거의 나오지 않음)

녹색은 → 또는 =

빨간색은 A 상자 | 파란색은 B 상자 | 색이 없는 글자는 부록

그래서 이런 문장 형태가 됩니다.

They call it 'Ghost Avenue' now. A→B=B′

★ 표가 붙은 문장은 다소 추상적인 표현을 사용한 문장입니다. 문장 형태를 확실히 이해하고 나서도 무슨 말인지 잘 와닿지 않을 수도 있습니다. 하지만 영어의 묘미가 듬뿍 담긴 문장이므로 천천히 음미해주길 바랍니다. 너무 어렵게 느껴지면 건너뛰고 읽어도 괜찮습니다.

일부 이해하기 어려운 문장은 바로 밑에 짧게나마 자세한 해설을 달아두었습니다.

3색사전은 스토리 부분의 영어 문장을 색깔로 구분하여 문장 형태를 한눈에 알아볼 수 있도록 만든 힌트북입니다. 물론 '정답'은 아닙니다. 영어 문장을 이해하기 위한 하나의 길잡이로 이용해주시기 바랍니다.

Something was wrong.   A=B

p.6

The owner knew this before he got the call.   A→B
> this는 앞 문장 전체의 대역입니다.

Because the young man, Ed Wishbone, had not returned to the office.   A↰

Maybe Ed Wishbone had been lying about the amount of money he had.
> A=B   lying에는 '거짓말하다'와 '눕다'란 두 가지 의미가 있어요. 여기서는 전자의 의미로 쓰였지만 p.14의 다섯 번째 문장에선 후자의 의미로 쓰였습니다.

Or maybe he had just changed his mind and walked away.   A=B and (A)↰

Young people are sometimes like that, especially nowadays.   A=B
> that은 앞 문장 전체의 대역입니다.

But the owner knew better.   A↰

He knew an honest man when he saw one.   A→B
> one은 an honest man의 대역입니다. an honest man을 see했을 때 그 사람이 honest man이라는 사실을 바로 know했다, 즉 알아차렸다는 의미지요. 종종 쓰이는 표현입니다.

Ed Wishbone was not a very sharp person, but he was definitely not a liar.
> A=B, but A=B   Sharp는 사람을 꾸미는 화장품으로도 쓰일 수 있어요.

And the fact that Jeremy Lightfoot's bodyguard stepped out of his office after Ed was not comforting at all.   A=B

So when the clinic called, the owner was not really surprised.   A=B

He just rushed over there.   A↰

The clinic was at the west end of the mall, along a narrow corridor between a hobby shop and a greeting card store.   A=B

p.7

Inside the clinic, the owner found a nurse standing in front of the door to the examining rooms.   A→B=B'

"Which room?" the owner asked.   A→B

"The one at the end of the hallway."   불완전한 문장

"What happened to him?"   A↺

"He was hit by a car.   A=B

His wounds are minor but we're worried about his head.   A=B, but A=B

He hit it pretty hard on the asphalt.   A→B
이 문장의 pretty는 '예쁘다, 귀엽다'란 의미가 아니라 '상당히'란 의미입니다. very보다
조금 약한 정도로 생각하면 딱 알맞아요.

We want to send him to the city hospital, but he won't go,"   A→B, but A↺

"Why not?"   불완전한 문장

"I'm not sure.   A=B

He may be confused from the shock.   A=B

Said something about looking for a cat.   (A)→B
대화문이므로 첫머리의 He는 생략했어요.

He wanted to leave but we stopped him.   A→B but A→B

He shouldn't even get out of bed yet."   A↺

p.8   The owner frowned and knocked on the door.   A↺ and (A)→B

When there was no answer, he opened it.   A→B

He was greeted by an ice-cold gust of wind.   A=B

"What the...? Mr. Wishbone?"   불완전한 문장

Wind was blowing in from an open window.   A=B

The curtains were flapping against the walls madly.   A=B

The owner ran to the window and poked his head out.   A↺ and (A)→B

"Mr. Wishbone!?"   불완전한 문장

★ **The November cold filled the darkness of the parking lot.**   A→B

　　cold가 darkness를 채우기란 물리적으로 불가능하지만, 그 이미지를 상상해보세요.

The only light came from the half moon above.   A↺

There was no sign of anyone anywhere.   A=B

　　이 문장에서의 sign은 신호나 간판을 가리키는 것이 아니라 '인기척'과 같은 의미입니다.

"Oh my God..."   불완전한 문장

p.9

I was late...   A=B

I was late again...   A=B

(But it wasn't my fault!)   A=B

p.10

I'm cold... got to find the cat... so cold...   A=B ... (A)→B

(Where am I?)   A=B

I'm a failure.   A=B

I've always been a failure.   A=B

(It was the cat's fault!)   A=B

Got to find the cat...   (A)→B

(so cold... so cold... so...)   불완전한 문장

p.11

cold...   불완전한 문장

p.13

p.14 "Son, you're gonna freeze to death if you sleep here," a voice said.   A→B

gonna는 going to의 줄임형입니다. 윌리가 애드를 son이라 부르며 친근하게 대하고 있네요.

It was a soft voice.   A=B

Ed moaned.   A↺

He was cold.   A=B

His cheek was lying on something hard.   A=B

"Son, you really better wake up."   A↺

Ed stirred and opened his eyes.   A↺ and (A)→B

His memory was a blur.   A=B

He didn't know where or when he was.   A→B

정확히 말하면 He didn't know where he was와 He didn't know when he was란 두 개의 문장입니다.

An old man was standing over him.   A=B

The man had a long white beard, very old skin, and eyes that reminded Ed of Santa Claus.   A→B

that 이하는 eyes의 화장문입니다. 이해하기 어려우면 that 이하를 like Santa Claus 로 바꿔보세요.

But it was a little too early for Santa, and Santa definitely didn't dress like this.   A=B, and A↺

p.15 "Son, I don't know what the heck you're doing here, but you better wake up if you don't wanna become a damn Popsicle."   A→B, but A↺

The old man moved slowly, pushing a baby stroller filled with books, magazines, and newspapers.   A↺

One of the wheels of the stroller was missing.   A=B

It had been replaced with the lid of a pot.   A=B

Ed got up with difficulty.   A↵

He was lying in a dark, dirty street.   A=B

The street was lined on both sides with buildings that had been closed for a
   long time.   A=B

It was quiet except for the rattle of the old man's stroller.   A=B

p.16

"Where am I?" **Ed said** in a weak voice.   A→B

His head was hurting like crazy.   A=B

"**You don't know** where you are?"   A→B

"**I think... I... I'm lost...**"   A→B

"**Damn right you are.**   A=B
   Damn은 right의 화장품입니다. 이 문장을 알기 쉽게 바꾸면 You are damn right.

Everyone who comes here is lost.   A=B

Pretty badly lost, as a matter of fact."   불완전한 문장
   a matter of fact는 직역하면 '사실상의 문제'로 단정적인 말투를 나타낼 때 덧붙여요.
   특별한 의미는 없는 상투적인 표현입니다.

Ed looked around again.   A↵

★ **The moon overhead cast shadows** into every corner.   A→B

A gust of wind blew down the street.   A↵

Ed just wanted to sleep.   A→B

He didn't want to walk anymore.   A→B

He had never been so tired in his whole life.   A=B

p.18

The old man walked over to a giant pile of junk by the side of the road.   A↻

The pile was made of stuff that had been thrown away when the street was still a part of the town.   A=B

stuff는 매우 편리한 단어입니다. 우리말로는 '물건이나 사물', '사람'을 대신해 부르는 '~것' 정도라고 생각하면 돼요.

"People have forgotten about this place.   A→B

They call it 'Ghost Avenue' now.   A→B=B'

We're just ghosts to them."   A=B

The old man picked a long piece of cloth that had probably been a curtain some decades ago.   A→B

He turned around to Ed and smiled.   A↻ and (A)↻

"We call it 'Treasure Island'."   A→B=B'

p.19

Ed blinked.   A↻

His blurry mind figured out that he was somewhere on the northwest side of town, near the old mines.   A→B

The area had been busy during the twenties and thirties because or the mining business.   A=B

The barber from the shop next to Pie Heaven had told him that there used to be a beautiful old cinema here.   A→B / B'

"Folks around here call me Willy. Professor Willy. Because I'm the only one who can read," the old man said.   A→B

He handed Ed the long piece of cloth.   A→B / B'

Ed took it reluctantly and wrapped it around himself.   A→B and (A)→B

It smelled bad.   A↻

"I...I'm Ed," he managed to say.   A→B

★ The light of the moon played with the shadows.   A↺

★ It was as if the street was alive.   A=B

"Nice to meet you, Ed. Now follow me," Willy said, and started down the
   street.   A→B, and (A)↺

Ed followed Willy slowly, walking deeper into the darkness of the street.
   A→B

Meanwhile, in another part of town...   불완전한 문장   p.20

And back in Ghost Avenue...   불완전한 문장   p.21

"Here we are," Willy said, stopping in front of a unique two-story structure.   p.22
   A→B

Ed looked up at the building in wonder.   A→B

It was a great big building.   A=B

The Old Everville Cinema really was beautiful.   A=B

The barber had not been kidding.   A=B

He had not been kidding about the 'old' part either.   A=B
   본문 19쪽에 나오는 barber가 'beautiful old cinema가 그곳에 있었다' 라고 한 문장을
   받아서 쓴 표현입니다. barber가 극장에 대해서 말했던 beautiful이나 old란 표현이 정
   확했으며 자신을 놀리지 않았단 사실을 깨닫고 에드가 쓴웃음을 짓고 있어요.

But the cinema still remained beautiful in a strange sort of way.   A→B
   sort는 '종류', way는 '방향'이에요. strange sort of way라면 '정상적인 방향에서 벗어
   나지만 기이하게도'라는 의미입니다.

"This used to be a great theater back in the fifties, you know. Big screen, great flicks, buttered popcorn... But that was a long time ago. Now it's our home," Willy said as he pushed open the doors of the once-glamorous theater.   A→B as A→B

p.23 Inside, the theater lobby was ruined.   A=B

The refreshment stand, the ticket booth, and the waiting area had been torn down, and everything had been replaced with piles of cardboard and miscellaneous junk.   A=B, and A=B

A few people were sitting there in the dark.   A=B

The only light inside was a lantern hung from the remains of a chandelier.   A=B

A man rummaging through a pile of soda cans looked up and grinned at Ed.   A↺ and (A)→B

"That's Frank," Willy said as he pushed his stroller through the mess.   A→B as A→B

"He won't hurt you.   A→B

Nice guy. Stinks, but a nice guy anyway."   불완전한 문장
줄이기 전 문장은 He stinks, but he is a nice guy anyway입니다.

"Howdy," Frank said to Ed, raising his hand awkwardly.   A→B
Howdy는 Hello의 변형이에요. 남부 시골 지방의 이미지를 풍기는 말투지요.

He had no teeth.   A→B

Ed just kept walking.   A→B

Willy walked across the lobby to a set of swinging doors that were hidden
   behind a broken vending machine.   A↺
   p.24
   swinging doors란 큰 회의장의 입구 등에서 흔히 볼 수 있는 여닫이문이에요.

Ed followed cautiously, glancing around the whole time.   A↺

The main part of the theater was better preserved than the lobby, except
   for one major difference.   A=B

There was a big hole in the ceiling.   A=B

The blue half moon shined through the hole, providing a soft light.   A↺

There was also a warm red glow from a small campfire that was burning
   directily underneath the hole.   A=B

"Here. Use them."   (A)→B
p.26

Willy pointed to a row of seats near the campfire.   A→B

Ed sat down.   A↺

He found the seats very mushy, but he didn't care.   A→B=B', but A↺

The seats were much better than the cold street outside.   A=B

"Well, you've met Frank, and that's George and Beejees.   A→B, and A=B

Louie's in that box over there, I don't know where Paddy is, but Marv's
   probably in the basement.   A=B, A→B but A=B
   Louie's와 Marv's는 Louie is와 Marv is의 줄임 형태입니다. 이 문장은 잘못 씌어진 문
   장이 아니에요. Louie는 실제로 상자에 들어가 있는 것입니다. 아마 그의 집일 거예요.

He almost never comes out."   A↺

Ed nodded.   A↺

"What do you do for a living, Ed?" Willy asked as he tossed a few crumpled-
p.27

up pieces of newspaper into the fire.　A→B as A→B

상대의 직업을 물을 때 쓰는 전형적인 표현입니다. living(생활)을 위해 do하는 것, 즉 '직업'이 무엇인지 윌리가 에드에게 묻고 있어요.

"I bake... I used to bake pies," Ed said, staring into the burning fire.　A→B

"That's a nice job."　A=B

"I lost my shop yesterday.　A→B

I'm not a baker anymore."　A=B

"Sure you are,　A=(B)

이해하기 쉽게 고쳐서 쓰면 You sure are a baker입니다.

You're just a baker without a shop."　A=B

p.28

"Not just my shop.　불완전한 문장

I lost my house, my savings, my bag, my whole life... all I have left is this."

A→B ... A=B　뒷부분은 A 상자를 발견하기 어려운 문장입니다. all I have left의 핵심 단어는 all이에요. left는 이 문장에서 '남겨진'이란 의미로 쓰인 화장품이고요. 이해하기 어려우면 left를 빼고 생각해보세요.

Ed took his rolling pin out of his coat pocket.　A→B

Somebody had found it lying near him in the parking lot of the New Mall.

A→B=B'

It always seemed to survive somehow.　A=B

Ed tossed it on the ground.　A→B

It rolled straight toward the fire.　A↺

It would have burned up if Willy hadn't reached out and grabbed it.　A↺

"Don't. This is important to you."　불완전한 문장　A=B

"No," Ed said.　A→B

"I'm really **not much of a baker**.   A=B
> 만약 이해하기 어렵다면 much of에 큰 의미는 없으므로 건너뛰고 읽어도 된답니다.

I just **like baking pies**.   A→B

I **was a mediocre salesman** until last year.   A=B

I **quit my job**, thinking I could become a pie baker because my mom used to bake great pies.   A→B

She **won a lot of contests**.   A→B

I **thought maybe I was like her**.   A→B

But **I wasn't. Stupid**."   A=(B)   **불완전한 문장**

Willy stood by the fire, listening with a faint smile on his face.   A⤸

★ **It was a smile worn** by time and hardened, almost petrified, by the **burdens of life**.   A=B
> 매우 어려운 문장입니다. worn은 '(옷을 오래도록 입어) 해지고 낡은 상태'를 말해요. 이 문장에서는 윌리의 웃음이 닳았다고 했지만 윌리 자신이라 생각해도 무방합니다. hardened와 petrified는 양쪽 다 '굳어지다'란 의미지만 petrified는 '화석'이 될만큼 딱 딱딱해진 상태를 가리켜요. 여기에 burdens를 '무거운 짐'이라고 생각하면 어떤 의미인지 이해가 되겠지요?

Ed continued to speak, the light of the fire playing on his face.   A→B

"**Mom** always **told me that life was like a blueberry pie**.   A→B / B'

Sometimes **it's sour** but most of the time **it's sweet**.   A=B but A=B

She **said the most wonderful thing in life was to eat a good, warm slice of pie**."   A→B

A tear formed at the corner of Ed's eye and **rolled** down his cheek.
> A⤸ but (A)⤸

"But **she was wrong**, you know.   A=B

p.31

She died of a heart attack when I was in high school.　A↺

From overwork.　불완전한 문장

My father had left us the year before, and she'd had to work two jobs to raise
　　me.　A→B, and A→B

One day when I came home from school, there was a slice of warm
　　blueberry pie on the table.　A=B

She was sitting in front of the oven, waiting for the pie to cool.　A=B

But... she wasn't breathing.　A=B

No last words.　불완전한 문장

I never even said 'thank you' to her.　A→B

I was too late.　A=B

I'm always too damn late."　A=B

Willy walked up to Ed and held the rolling pin out to him.　A↺ and (A)→B

Ed shook his head, tears streaming down his face.　A→B

"No. I'm not going to bake any more pies.　A=B

Life isn't a blueberry pie.　A=B

A child can see that.　A→B

It's... It's... more like a mustard pie."　A=B

"Look, Ed.　A↺

You're going to get a good night's sleep. and then in the morning. you're
　　going to go back to your life.　A=B, and A=B

You are not one of us.　A=B

You have a life.　A→B

Go back to it."　(A)↺

"You don't understand.　A↺

I can't bake pies like my mother.　A→B

I don't have it in me.   A→B

it은 'bake pies like my mother'의 대역으로 엄마처럼 파이를 구울 수 있는 재능을 의미해요.

I was only pretending I could."   A=B

"That's because you have no idea what a pie is really made of."   A=B

That은 세 문장 앞 'I can't ~'로 시작하는 문장 전체의 대역입니다.

have no idea도 일상 회화에서 자주 쓰이는 관용 표현이에요. "전혀 모른다"는 의미를 완곡하게 나타낸 표현이지요.

"Sure I do.   A↩

do를 이해하기 어려우면 know로 바꿔보세요.

I use the same things my mother did.   A→B

I even use the same brand of flour.   A→B

It doesn't make any difference."   A→B

It은 바로 앞에 나오는 두 문장의 내용을 가리키는 대역입니다.

"You had a great mom.   A→B

She understood life well.   A→B

She knew why pies were important.   A→B

That's why she was a great baker."   A=B

That은 앞 문장의 대역입니다.

"Pies are just pies.   A=B

Thay're not important."   A=B

p.32

A long silent moment passed.   A↩

Ed looked away while Willy tended the fire.   A↩

★ **The crackling sounds of the fire eating into the wood filled the air.**   A→B

이 문장의 표현도 상당히 시적입니다.

Finally, Willy spoke.　A⤴

His voice was slow and calm.　A=B

"Most of us haven't had a slice of pie in years, Ed."　A→B

Ed stopped wiping his tears.　A→B

Still wearing that faint and petrified smile, Willy continued, "Take Frank
　　for example. He's been here for more than ten years now. He's
　　probably forgotten what a pie looks like."　A→B

"Willy gestured toward Frank, who was now near the campfire, looking for
something in another big pile of junk.　A⤴
　　who는 Frank의 대역입니다.

"Why doesn't he just buy one?" Ed said with a rather guilty look on his face.
　　A→B

"I mean, he could get a job, couldn't he?　A→B

A pie is just a buck or so.　A=B

Frank chose to be here... just like me.　A→B

Bad luck, but it's probably his own fault.　A=B

Anybody can buy a piece of pie.　A→B

You just need to go out and..."　A→B

At that moment, Frank moved toward the fire.　A⤴

Ed suddenly noticed that he had no legs.　A→B

p.34 The tears came back all at once.　A⤴

Ed's face turned red and he covered his mouth with his hand.
　　A⤴ and A→B　　turned는 이 문장에서 '돌아가다'란 의미가 아니라 '변화하다'란 의미
입니다.

The tears streamed over his hand.　A⤴

"I'm... I'm so sorry.　A=B

I didn't mean... oh no...　A→(B)

I'm... I'm so sorry.　A=B

I'm so confused...　A=B

I'm really, really sorry..."　A=B

"No harm done, Ed," Willy said.　A→B
이 문장도 회화에서 자주 쓰이는 표현이에요. harm은 '해', '해가 없다'고 썼지만 문맥상 '신경 쓰지 않아도 된다'는 의미입니다.

"Frank was born on the street.　A=B
on the street는 문자 그대로 '길에서 태어났다'는 의미가 아니라 일정한 거처 없이 떠돌아 다니는 부모 밑에서 태어났다는 의미입니다.

Never knew his parents...　(A)→B

A car hit him when he was twenty.　A→B

Three hospitals refused to treat him and he ended up here."　A→B and A↺

★ The soft light of the moon enveloped the theater in its warm glow.　A→B

★ The smoke from the campfire rose through the hole in the ceiling, up toward the sky, where it scattered among the clouds.　A↺

★ The whole theater seemed like a gentle shelter for life.　A=B

"Ed... most of us here will die without eating another piece of pie... and we're the luckier ones.　A↺... and A=B
p.35

Some people never have the chance to eat pie.　A→B
Some people이 eat pie할 기회를 전혀 가져보지 못했다, 다시 말해 '한번도 먹어보지 못했다'는 뜻입니다. 그다음 문장은 'lives(인생)'에서 그런 기회가 한번도 없었다는 의미로 앞 문장을 한층 강조합니다.

Not once in their lives.　불완전한 문장

Some people have never had anything sweet, not in their mouths or in their hearts.   A→B

For those people, Ed, life isn't a blueberry pie or a mustard pie.   A=B

Life is just hell."   A=B

Willy put the rolling pin down on the seat beside Ed and turned toward the campfire again.   A→B and (A)↺

"Sleep, Ed.   A↺

Then go back.   (A)↺

Bake more pies."   (A)→B

p.36

And it was a long night.   A=B

The longest night of Ed's life.   불완전한 문장

He was as tired as possible, but he still could not sleep.   A=B, but A↺

He watched the campfire burn down.   A→B=B'

He watched the moon shining in the sky.   A→B=B'

And he watched the "ghosts" of Everville sleeping in their beds of garbage.
   A→B=B'

Garbage that he might have thrown away.   불완전한 문장
   이 문장에서 he는 이전의 에드를 가리켜요.

He thought about all the pies he had baked.   A→B

He thought even more about the many pies he had thrown away.   A→B

p.37

He thought of his mother.   A→B

He thought of his mother a lot that night.   A→B

Life is like a blueberry pie, Eddie.   A=B

　　Eddie는 Ed의 애칭이에요.

Sometimes it's sour, but most of the time, it's sweet.   A=B, but A=B

For the first time in ten years, Ed remembered that there was something after those words.   A→B

　　those words는 앞에 나오는 이탤릭체 문장인 Life is ~ it's sweet을 가리켜요. 에드가 이 문장 뒤(after)에 숨겨진 의미(something)를 깨달았다는 뜻이지요. 그 숨은 의미는 뒤에 나오는 이탤릭체 문장 It's always ~ you love입니다.

Perhaps the most important part which he had forgotten a long time ago.

　　불완전한 문장

And you know what, Eddie?   A→B

It's always sweet if you eat it witch the people you love.   A=B

Ed cried himself to sleep, and in the morning, he knew what he had to do.

　　A→B, and A→B

When Willy woke up that morning, he couldn't believe what he smelled.

　　A→B

p.38

It was the smell of fresh-baked pie.   A=B

　　이 문장의 It은 앞 문장에 나온 what he smelled의 대역입니다.

It was something he hadn't smelled for a long, long time.   A=B

　　이 두 문장의 It도 앞 문장에 나온 what he smelled의 대역이네요.

Willy got up and found his fellow ghosts standing around the campfire with Ed.   A↫ and (A)→B=B'

Ed was slicing up an apple pie.   A=B

　　up은 '마무리'를 나타내는 접착제입니다. 그리 중요한 의미는 없지만 의외로 쓰일 때가 많은 단어지요. slicing만으로는 한 번만 칼집을 넣어 잘랐다는 의미가 되므로, 여러 번 칼집을 넣어서 완전히 잘라냈다는 의미를 나타내기 위해 up을 썼어요.

p.40

"I'll be darned," Willy mumbled, his eyes wids with astonishment.   A→B

조금 유행에 뒤진 듯한 표현이지만 '도저히 당해낼 수 없군!' 혹은 '내가 졌다!'라는 의미로 또래의 남자들이 자주 쓰는 표현입니다.

A metal container was hanging over the campfire, and more pies were baking inside of it.   A=B, and A=B

Ed saw Willy and spoke to hime with a smile.   A→B and (A)↻

"I only had enough money for apple jam, so I guess it's not a genuine apple pie.   A→B, so A→B

And the crust is just graham crackers.   A=B

graham crackers는 단맛이 도는 크래커로 잘게 부수어 파이 반죽으로 쓰면 맛있어요. 살짝 구운 머시멜로를 크래커 사이에 끼워서 한번 먹어보세요. 감동적인 맛이에요.

But I did the best I could.   A→B

이해가 잘 가지 않을 때는 I did my best로 바꿔도 상관없어요.

I saved you a big piece. Here."   A→B / B'

p.41

Willy took the slice of apple pie from Ed.   A→B

It was on a piece of wax paper.   A=B

No fork, no napkin, but it was really apple pie.   A=B

"You were right. I guess I am a baker after all," Ed said.   A→B

이 문장에서의 all은 지금까지 에드의 신상에 일어난 모든 사건을 가리키는 대역입니다.. after all은 그 모든 것들 후에, 즉 '결국'이라는 뜻이에요.

Willy bit into the pie.   A→B

It was sweet.   A=B

It smelled of a long time ago.   A↻

"Thank you," Willy said with a big smile.   A→B

Ed smiled back and said, "I'm going to get some more wax paper."
  A⤴ and (A)→B

"Sure. Oh, Paddy's probably out in front of the theater sweeping.   A=B
  Paddy's는 Paddy is를 줄인 형태입니다.

Please give him a slice too."   (A)→B / B'

"Okay, I'll look for him," Ed said, and stepped out of the theater.
  A→B, and (A)⤴

But Paddy wasn't there.   A=B p.42
  이 페이지는 조금 어려우므로 본문 p.42의 해설에 해당하는 '퍼즐 맞추기' 부분에서 자세
  히 설명했습니다.

Instead, Ed saw a big black man standing by the side of Ghost Avenue.
  A→B=B'

The man's eyes were searching for something.   A=B

Ed froze, the slice of apple pie held in his hand.   A⤴

He recognized the man from somewhere.   A→B

The man looked like the bodyguard who had been standing behind the rich
  man at the New Mall's office.   A=B
  looked를 이해하기 어렵다면 seemed로 바꿔서 읽어보세요.

He also looked a lot like the man who had grabbed his bag.   A=B
  이 문장도 마찬가지예요. looked를 이해하기 어렵다면 seemed로 바꿔서 읽어보세요.

At that moment, the man's eyes met Ed's eyes, and Ed suddenly knew what
  the man had been searching for.   A→B, and A→B

Because the man had just found it.   A→B

p.43

Ed started to turn around, but it was too late.　A→B but A=B

The man seized Ed from behind and slammed him against the outside wall of the theater.　A→B and (A)→B

"No words," the man whispered to Ed as he held him against the wall.　A→B as A→B

Completely terrified, Ed was unable to speak anyway.　A=B

"Understand?" the man whispered again.　A→B

Ed nodded desperately, although he could not understand what was happening at all.　A↺, although A→B

He could barely breathe.　A↺

The giant black man stuffed a piece of paper in Ed's mouth and said just two more words.　A→B and (A)→B

"Sign it."　(A)→B

이 문장에서 sign은 '서명하다'라는 의미입니다. 서명을 하는 것도 결국 '흔적'이나 '표시' 를 남기는 것이므로 sign이 '서명하다'라는 의미도 지니게 돼요.

Ed nodded at once.　A↺

It was the only thing he could do.　A=B

It은 'nod하는 것' 자체를 말해요.

p.44

The man let him go.　A→B=B'

Ed dropped to his knees on the ground, the pie falling from his hand.　A↺

The man tossed a pen at Ed, and then started walking back to the limousine.
A→B, and (A)→B　toss도 throw도 의미는 '던지다'이지만 던지는 방법에 약간 차이 가 있어요. throw는 위에서 내리치는 인상이 있는 반면, toss는 아래에서 가볍게 위로 쳐 올리는 이미지입니다.

Shaking all over, Ed picked up the pen and started signing his name.
A→B and (A)→B

He couldn't think.   A↩

He was too scared.   A=B

Before he finished signing his name, the sound of the limousine door rang in
his ear.   A↩

Ed raised his eyes from the ground and saw something that made his blood
run cold.   A→B and (A)→B

The man was holding Ed's bag.   A=B

And something was stuffed inside.   A=B

Something very still. Something shaped like a big, fat cat.   불완전한 문장

The man came back, and set the bag down in front of Ed.   A↩, and (A)→B   p.45

Then the man picked up the paper.   A→B

He checked the signature quickly, and without even a glance at Ed, started
back to the limousine.   A→B, and (A)↩

Ed's heart was bouncing in his chest.   A=B

He hed the urge to throw up but he pushed it back.   A→B but A→B
영어로 '토하다'는 vomit이지만, 이 단어는 지저분한 느낌이 들므로 좀 더 완곡한 표현을
써서 'throw up'이라고 했어요. 우리말로도 '토하다'라고 하지 않고 '넘어오다'라고 완곡
하게 말하는 경우가 있잖아요. 마찬가지 뉘앙스로 때에 따라 구분해서 쓰면 좋습니다.
It은 '구토증'의 대역이에요.

He remembered thinking that all of his problems were the cat's fault.
A→B

"Oh, cat... I'm sorry... I'm so sorry..."   A=B ... A=B

Ed slowly pulled the zipper of the bag open.   A→B

p.46

"AAAGGGGGHHHHHH!!" 불완전한 문장

Ed shouted as a very frustrated cat popped out of the bag with a snarl and scratched his face.   A⊃ as A⊃ and (A)→B

The cat leaped aside, and almost immediately noticed the piece of pie on the ground.   A⊃, and (A)→B

The cat took a giant stretch, and with the grace that only cats possess, approached the pie and started to devour it.   A→B, and (A)→B and (A)→B
grace는 매우 기품있는 모습을 표현하는 단어지만, devour는 게걸스럽게 먹는 모습을 나타내요. 이런 믹스매치가 고양이란 동물의 본질일지도 모르죠.

p.47

A smile of relief appeared on Ed's face, as he sat down on the sidewalk weakly.   A⊃, as A⊃

The limousine had already driven away.   A⊃

Ed leaned against the wall of the theater and let out a deep breath.
A⊃ and (A)→B

He still couldn't understand what that had been all about.   A→B
이 문장에 쓰인 that은 지금까지 일어난 일련의 '다툼'을 나타내는 대역입니다.

It was probably something about the vacant space in the mall, but he didn't care anymore.   A=B, but A⊃
이 문장에 쓰인 it은 지금까지 일어난 일련의 '다툼'을 나타내는 대역입니다.

He was just glad that it was over.   A=B
이 문장에 쓰인 it은 지금까지 일어난 일련의 '다툼'을 나타내는 대역입니다.
over는 소위 game over라고 할 때의 over와 마찬가지로 '종료 지점을 통과했다'는 의미입니다.

The cat finished the piece of pie and looked up at Ed for more.
A→B and (A)→B

It seemed dissatisfied, maybe because the pie was not blueberry.   A=B

"You understand a lot more than you seem to, don't you, cat?" Ed asked.

A→B　이해하기 어려울 경우에는 than you seem to를 건너뛰고 읽어도 돼요.

A weak but sincere smile spread across his face.　A↺

"Blueberry pie is the only pie I still make from my mom's original recipe."

A=B

Ed looked into the cat's eyes.　A→B

The cat looked back.　A↺

It was a weird but pleasant moment, there on the sidewalk of a forgotten town.　A=B

One cat and its owner, just staring at each other awkwardly.　불완전한 문장

Then, after a long silent moment, the cat burped.　A↺

"Ugh! That's horrible," Ed laughed.　A→B

The cat made a annoyed face and started to look for somewhere warm to take a nap.　A→B, and (A)→B

It still seemed hungry.　A=B

★ Ed's laughter echoed down the wide, empty road of Ghost Avenue, up and down, over and below, and on into the first glimpse of the day ahead.　A↺

Ed Wishbone knew that the rest of his life had begun.　A→B

3권을 끝내며

멀리 있는 목표를 향해 걸어갈 때는 단계별로 작은 목표를 세워두면 도움이 된다고 합니다. 이런 노력 덕분에 3권도 무사히 끝낼 수 있었습니다. 아직 시행착오도 많고 여전히 요령도 부족하지만, 여러 가지 의미에서 이번 작품은 하나의 분기점이 될 듯합니다.

자, 인생의 고비를 맞이한 에드는 앞으로 어떻게 될까요? 물론 에드의 인생도, 고양이와 함께하는 영어 여행도 계속 이어집니다. 특히 이번 작품을 통해 에드의 내면에는 변화가 일어났습니다. 그와 동반해서 해설의 수준도 한 단계 올라갔습니다. 작은 목표를 달성한 셈이지요.

우리가 살아가는 현실도 에드의 인생과 비슷합니다. 한치 앞을 알 수 없고 오직 자신의 힘으로 걸어가야만 하는 세상에 살고 있지요. 물론 두려울 때도 있지만 전진하지 않으면 어디에도 갈 수 없습니다. 지금 현재 처해 있는 이 상황에 그냥 머물러 있으면 안 될까 하고 생각하는 사람도 있겠지요. 하지만 어떻게든 앞으로 걸어가야 합니다. 바로 에드처럼.

그러나 앞으로 나아갈 때도 기본 원칙은 있습니다.

어른이 되면 현실 속의 하루하루는 마치 제트코스터처럼 휘익 지나가버립니다. 그리고 그 제트코스터 같은 속도에 발맞춰 살아간다고 해도 원하는 걸 모두 얻을 수는 없습니다. 욕심을 부려봤자 한줌의 모래처럼 손가락 사이로 새어나가버리지요. 욕심은 버리고 꾸준히 전진해야 합니다. 영어 읽기도 인생처럼 장기전입니다. 너무 욕심만 부리다 보면 빨리 지치게 됩니다. 멀리 보며 묵묵히 걸어나가야 하죠. 우리가 도달해야 할 목표는 영어 암기가 아니라 영어를 구사해서 세계로 향하는 것이니까요.

세계로 향하는 그 길에 에드와 빅팻캣이 함께할 겁니다. 그리고 이번 작품으로 이미 여러분은 작은 목표를 달성했습니다. 그러므로 지금까지 함께한 친구 분들은 자신에게 박수를 쳐주었으면 합니다. 얼마 전만 해도 영어책을 읽는다는 것은 상상조차 못했던 친구도 있으리라고 생각합니다. 당시를 떠올리면서 '아직도 영어를 못하는 자신'을 질책하기보다는 '어떻게 해서든 여기까지 온 자신'에게 조촐한 축하인사를 해주었으면 합니다.

영어 여행은 계속됩니다. 하지만 적어도 하나의 분기점까지 왔습니다. 그리고 이는 분명 멋진 일입니다.

Good luck and happy reading!
Takahiko Mukoyama

이 시리즈는 영문법 교재가 아닙니다. 학습서도 아닙니다. '영어 읽기'를 최우선 목표로 삼고 쓴 책입니다. 몸으로 체험하고 느낄 수 있도록 기존 영문법과는 조금 다른 해석을 실은 부분도 있습니다. 어디까지나 이제 막 영어 읽기를 시작하는 학생들의 이해를 돕기 위해서 의도적으로 도입한 장치들입니다.

STAFF

written and produced by Takahiko Mukoyama	기획 · 원작 · 글 · 해설 무코야마 다카히코
illustrated by Tetsuo Takashima	그림 · 캐릭터 디자인 다카시마 데츠오
translated by Eun Ha Kim	우리말 번역 김은하
art direction by Yoji Takemura	아트 디렉터 다케무라 요지
technical advice by Fumika Nagano	테크니컬 어드바이저 나가노 후미카
edited by Will Books Editorial Department	편집 윌북 편집부
English-language editing by Michael Keezing	영문 교정 마이클 키징
supportive design by Will Books Design Department	디자인 협력 윌북 디자인팀
supervised by Atsuko Mukoyama Yoshihiko Mukoyama	감수 무코야마 아츠코(梅光学院大学) 무코야마 요시히코(梅光学院大学)
a studio ET CETERA production	제작 스튜디오 엣세트러
published by Will Books Publishing Co.	발행 윌북

special thanks to:

Mac & Jessie Gorham
Baiko Gakuin University

series dedicated to "Fuwa-chan", our one and only special cat

Studio ET CETERA는 야마구치현 시모노세키시에서 중학교 시절을 함께 보낸 죽마고우들이 의기투합하여 만든 기획 집단입니다. 우리 스튜디오는 작가, 프로듀서, 디자이너, 웹마스터 등 다재다능한 멤버들로 구성되어 있으며 주로 출판 분야에서 엔터테인먼트와 감성이 결합된 작품을 만드는 것을 목표로 하고 있습니다.
ET CETERA라는 이름은 어떤 분류에도 속할 수 있으면서 동시에 어떤 분류에도 온전히 속하지 않는 '그 외'라는 뜻의 et cetera에서 따왔습니다. 우리들만이 할 수 있는 독특한 작품을 만들겠다는 의지의 표현이자 '그 외'에 속하는 많은 사람들을 위해 작품을 만들겠다는 소망이 담긴 이름입니다.

옮긴이 **김은하**

유년 시절을 일본에서 보낸 추억을 잊지 못해 한양대학교에서 일어일문학을 전공했다. 어려서부터 한일 양국의 언어를 익힌 덕분에 번역이 천직이 되었다. 번역하는 틈틈이 바른번역 글밥 아카데미에서 출판 번역 강의를 겸하고 있다. 주요 역서로 〈클래식, 나의 뇌를 깨우다〉, 〈지구 온난화 충격 리포트〉, 〈세계에서 제일 간단한 영어책〉, 〈빅팻캣의 영어 수업: 영어는 안 외우는 것이다〉 등 다수가 있다.

Big Fat Cat and the Ghost Avenue

빅팻캣과 고스트 애비뉴 빅팻캣 시리즈 3

펴낸날 개정판 1쇄 2018년 5월 20일
　　　　개정판 5쇄 2024년 5월 24일
글작가 무코야마 다카히코
그림작가 다카시마 데츠오
옮긴이 김은하

펴낸이 이주애, 홍영완
펴낸곳 (주)윌북
출판등록 제2006-000017호

주소 10881 경기도 파주시 광인사길 217
전자우편 willbooks@naver.com
전화 031-955-3777
팩스 031-955-3778
홈페이지 willbookspub.com
블로그 blog.naver.com/willbooks 포스트 post.naver.com/willbooks
트위터 @onwillbooks 인스타그램 @willbooks_pub

ISBN 979-11-5581-167-2 14740